100 IDEAS
FOR TEACHING HISTORY

CONTINUUM ONE HUNDREDS SERIES

100 Ideas for Managing Behaviour – Johnnie Young
100 Ideas for Teaching Citizenship – Ian Davies
100 Ideas for Teaching Creativity – Stephen Bowkett
100 Ideas for Teaching History – Julia Murphy
100 Ideas for Teaching Languages – Nia Griffith
100 Ideas for Teaching Mathematics – Mike Ollerton

OTHER HISTORY TITLES

Teaching History 3–11 – Mark O'Hara and Lucy O'Hara
Reflective Teaching of History 11–18 – Rob Phillips

100 IDEAS
FOR TEACHING
HISTORY

Julia Murphy

continuum
LONDON • NEW YORK

Continuum International Publishing Group

The Tower Building   15 East 26th Street
11 York Road   New York
London   NY 10010
SE1 7NX

www.continuumbooks.com

© Julia Murphy 2005

British Library Cataloguing-in-Publication Data

A catalogue record for this book is available from the British
Library.

ISBN: 0–8264–8493–X (paperback)

Designed and typeset by Ben Cracknell Studios | Janice Mather

Printed and bound in Great Britain by MPG Books Ltd, Bodmin

CONTENTS

SECTION 3 **Understanding chronology**

SECTION 4 **Written activities**

SECTION 5 **Drama activities**

SECTION 6 Using Information and Communication Technology

SECTION 7 Using primary sources

SECTION 11 **Plenary activities and homework**

SECTION 12 **The value of money throughout the ages**

SECTION 13 **At your fingertips**

The ideas in this book have been arranged not by topic area, but instead there's a skills-based approach. The reason for this is simple: history, unlike subjects such as mathematics, is not solely based on accumulated knowledge. You don't need to have grasped the burial practices of the ancient Egyptians to study Tudor Britain, for example. There are varying national curricula for history, and within this there are choices of units to study.

Throughout this book, therefore, many of the tips give you examples of how you could incorporate the ideas into specific topics of study, from Key Stage 1 to Key Stage 3. Many of the tips can be adapted to any topic studied in history.

Using the same teaching techniques and exercises throughout a child's education is said to ease transitions between schools, so that primary children who may be used to making models, painting portraits and other creative approaches to history, are not shocked by sudden requests to write extended answers once they reach secondary school.

These methods also allow pupils to develop skills, such as essay writing, that are transferable to other subjects. If writing frames are introduced early enough, the structures can gradually be removed, so that ideally many pupils will end up writing structured pieces without any need for prompts.

Hopefully you'll find that you can pick and choose from the ideas offered here, and adapt them to your own particular needs and preferences. I don't claim originality in all these ideas: many of them have been tried and tested for many years in classrooms across Britain; for these I am indebted to colleagues past and present. But they should provide non-specialists, and those new to the profession, with a host of teaching techniques and classroom ideas collected together in one handy guide.

Making history relevant

Why do we study history? A book of teaching ideas is not the place to start a discussion that has preoccupied scholars for many years and through many tomes of academic study. But this is a question you'll be asked by pupils who haven't yet made a connection between what they are studying and their own lives. The best way to tackle this question is to anticipate it, and have regular reminders around your classroom that show the importance of history.

This is not a contribution to the academic debate, but here are some reasons you can give your pupils when they ask you that question.

1   You get to learn about what it was like in the past. Ever wondered what life was like before computers? How old your house is? What it was like before going to school was the law? Why going to school became the law? What would you be doing right now if you lived in the past? Why we celebrate Bonfire Night and Mothering Sunday? Why we have castles and standing stones and strange unnatural mounds of earth? Or even just why we have football matches on Saturday afternoons?

  If you turn the questions on the pupils, you can really start to fire their imaginations. It's even better if you can relate it to local buildings, parks or features in your area.

2   It lets you learn how to think. You are able to ask questions and use evidence to draw conclusions. You can weigh up different sides to stories. You get to see what happens when people make decisions that affect hundreds or thousands of people, and decide if you think they made the right decision.

The previous idea suggested a couple of ways to answer the question 'why do we study history?' Here follow three more responses that could help your pupils to understand why history is relevant. You could use them as a basis for a classroom display. Encourage pupils to bring in examples to add to your display, for example a postcard from a castle they've visited, or even an advert they've torn from a magazine. So why do we study history?

1 You learn about things that are happening in the world today. For example, you find out why some countries are friendly towards each other and why some are at war.
2 You get to practise skills that you need for other school subjects, like writing detailed answers and essays, putting together an argument and using different sources to construct your own work. These skills will help you to read newspapers and watch the news on television, because you'll understand that there's more than one side to every story.
3 You'll become a more informed person. You'll start to understand the historical references that crop up everywhere, from Hollywood blockbusters to episodes of *The Simpsons* and via adverts. You probably already know lots more about history than you realize, whether you enjoy playing computer games like 'Age of Empires', or you've visited a castle on holiday. Learning history at school lets you learn more about all the historical things that surround us.

As a teacher, you'll probably be able to add more answers to pacify your pupils, especially those that relate to the topics you're studying. Just make sure you're prepared for the questions!

FURTHER REASONS TO STUDY HISTORY

DISPLAYING PUPILS' WORK

Wall displays may be slipping out of the realm of the teacher's responsibilities, but you should still use the opportunity to create a pleasant and relevant working environment in your room. There are many different things you could use for display purposes, and what follows are just a few suggestions.

You could pre-empt the question 'why do we study history?' by covering your wall with statements about the value of history, similar to those mentioned in the previous sections.

Choose a theme for each half term. If you're a primary teacher, this will be the topic you're currently studying. If you teach lots of different classes in a secondary school, you might choose to rotate your displays between different year groups. This can often capture the imaginations of younger pupils, who see some of the things they will be doing in the next year, and so remain enthusiastic about the subject. It can also make the older pupils feel nostalgic, as they tell you they remember when they studied castles or the Black Death.

You can include bright and colourful work produced by the pupils, examples of the type of work they need to do to attain a certain grade or level, key vocabulary, posters or pictures that they may have seen reproduced in their textbooks and website addresses and book titles for those interested in finding out more.

If you take a trip to a historical site, make sure you take a digital camera too. Then you can create a picture record of your visit, and most children enjoy seeing themselves and their classmates up on the wall. Add leaflets and postcards to the display and project work produced as a result of the visit. Including the personal touch encourages other classes to scrutinize the display too.

You could create displays relevant to the time of year. What better time to explain the Gunpowder Plot than the beginning of November? Or you could cover science and superstition around Hallowe'en time. Then move on to explain why we wear poppies for 11 November. At Christmas, you could show how Christmas is celebrated throughout the ages, or concentrate on a Tudor or Restoration Christmas. It could be an opportunity to draw upon other cultures and multicultural celebrations, especially if you could tie it in with the Aztecs or ancient Egyptians, for example.

Timelines are a great way of showing and explaining chronology. There's more information about these in Section 3 – Understanding Chronology.

For older pupils, especially near the time when they're choosing their options, you could make a small display showing lots of famous people who have history degrees. Start collecting quotations if you chance across them, where celebrities mention their love of history or what they're particularly interested in. Once you start looking, the topic crops up quite often!

THIS DAY IN HISTORY

This is a great way to show change and continuity to the pupils on a regular basis, and to encourage them to seek out information. It also shows them that history includes so much more than the topics they study at school. A nice touch, especially in primary schools, is to include any class birthdays in this activity, adding the year in which the pupil was born.

All you need is a small space of your classroom wall with a permanent 'This day in history' title. You could ask a member of your class to find out about an event that happened any number of years ago, or you could invest in one of the cheap books or calendars that will helpfully have done your research for you. There are websites, such as the BBC's history section, that have the same idea.

You could have it displayed on your wall as merely a curiosity, or you could use the event as a springboard for further discussion, such as how does that event affect us today, if at all? Or if you want to test your pupils' grasp of chronology, ask them to place the event on a timeline, or simply ask them whether it comes before or after the last 'This day in history' display that they saw.

This is another way of showing that there's more to history than the topics covered in lessons, although newspaper articles often do tie in with topics you're studying, whether they are about Remembrance Day or a new tomb found in Egypt. Finding articles from a wide range of newspapers also shows the pupils how they are surrounded by references to history.

Local papers may report on new archaeological discoveries and thrive on old photos of the locality. They often have their own sections on what the headlines were 50 or 100 years ago, and readers send in photos they find in their attics, for example asking for more information on the people in the school photo with their grandparents. All these reproduced photos are a goldmine for covering local history, especially if you teach in a locality that's new to you.

National papers have their uses too. Some of the broadsheets have correspondents for archaeology, while the tabloids can only be commended for bringing humour to the subject. My recent favourites from the tabloids included an article about an Egyptian mummy, whose headline was 'The Bling King', which certainly made the pupils look. Then there was the artist who decided to draw the reconstructed prehistoric settlement near Newcastle with the people wearing tunics in Newcastle United's football colours. Such articles can certainly be a starting point for discussion!

This is an extra-curricular activity, perhaps one for a form group or history club. Sometimes it can tie in with the topics you're covering in lessons.

Display a picture of a famous historical figure that is currently being used in an advertising campaign, TV series, blockbuster film or who has been in the news for some reason. Alternatively, take in pictures of some notable person whose statue is in the school's locality. Set up an investigation to find out more about this historical figure, and pin the findings around the picture. Even those pupils who are less than enthusiastic about lessons will notice a picture on your wall of 'that bloke off the telly' and may peer a bit closer.

You could do this challenge in reverse too. Display a silhouetted picture with a big question mark in the middle, and leave clues around the picture as to the person's identity. You could add a few more clues each week over a half term, and challenge everyone who uses your classroom to work out who the mysterious figure is.

If you have space, dedicate a corner of the room to artefacts. Pupils can bring in old objects to form part of an investigation. They could guess what the object is, and have a go at drawing it accurately, describing it and categorizing it. If the objects are from different eras, you can use them in a variety of ways: to compare and contrast; to show change and continuity; or to place on a three-dimensional timeline. With more unusual objects, you could have a 'call my bluff' type of quiz, where different pupils argue strongly for the rest to support their claims to the object's use.

You can gather objects related to your current topic of study. If it's a recent period of history, pupils may find objects like ration books, old letters, old coins and stamps, and even gas masks and medals at home. Your local education authority or museum may have an artefacts loan system, where you borrow some relevant objects for a few weeks. Otherwise, get your class to be creative and make their own jewellery, masks, dolls, model pyramids, and so on, which can then be displayed in your classroom museum. This may be something to get an extra-curricular history club involved in if you don't have time in lessons.

Lesson starter activities

GENERAL TIPS

These days, there's a lot more to history than learning facts and figures by rote. Pupils should be developing thinking skills, such as the ability to analyse. However, to grasp chronological understanding, as the National Curriculum expects each pupil to do from Key Stage 1 upwards, as well as accumulating knowledge and understanding of events, people and changes in the past, there's no substitute for learning key words, names and dates. These are the springboard from which the history student dives into the deeper waters of analysis.

Lesson starter activities allow your class to become settled and focused on the subject. This is especially important in secondary schools, where pupils may trickle into the room from various locations around the school. A starter activity gives pupils time to recall what they learned from the previous history lesson, which may have been several days and many lessons ago. It also gives pupils who may have missed a lesson 5 or 10 minutes to catch up with any reading they need to do.

Get the pupils into the habit of coming into the classroom, getting out all the things they need for the lesson, and then either working on an independent starter activity from the selection which follows that you've displayed on the board, or revising their notes from the previous lesson in preparation for the starter you're about to explain. This way, even if pupils turn up to your lessons in trickles, everyone has something purposeful to be working on while you wait for the stragglers.

SEQUENCE THE PAST

This starter is great for reinforcing chronological understanding. You can even use it if you don't have any time to prepare it in advance. If you want to prepare, select four or five pictures based on events you've previously studied. Provide pupils with photocopies, or display them on your board. For example, you could have different parts of the Bayeux Tapestry if you're studying the Battle of Hastings. If you're studying World War I, you could have pictures of a man enlisting, being equipped and being sent to the front line. For the ancient Egyptians, you might have the stages of building a pyramid or the more gruesome process of mummification. Pupils rearrange these pictures in order.

If you haven't prepared, you can still use this starter, by writing four or five events out of sequence on the board, and asking pupils to rearrange them in chronological order.

If you use pictures, the pupils can write captions to go with each one. If you use written events, ask the pupils to provide an event to go before and after the correctly arranged sequence.

A useful way of reinforcing words learned in the previous lesson is to start with a game of bingo. Your department may give pupils a vocabulary list at the start of each topic, term or year which contains words specific to your subject. Or you may have key terms displayed on your classroom wall. You can use these, or you could simply write up a list of 10 or 15 words associated with your unit of study. New vocabulary should be introduced gradually: don't confuse the pupils by suddenly writing up a list of a dozen new words!

Once you have given the pupils a list of words to choose from, tell them to write down six of them on a piece of paper. This is now their bingo card. For younger children, you could choose one of the words to read out, and if they have it on their card, they can cross it off. The first pupil to cross off all six of their words calls out 'bingo' and is declared the winner. If you need a tie-breaker, perhaps use it as a chance to develop literacy and ask them to spell the words back to you without looking.

For children in Key Stages 2 and 3, bingo can become a more thoughtful activity. Once they have selected their six words from the list you provide, you can give them definitions of the words to work out before crossing them off on their lists. For example, in a unit on the ancient Egyptians, this could range from a simple definition, such as 'this building was used to hold the bodies and belongings of dead pharaohs', to the more taxing. To stretch the more able, provide clues of a more cryptic nature. If you teach mixed ability, start off each definition with a difficult clue, and then gradually reveal more information so that eventually each pupil has access to the answer.

Bingo can be played using key dates too. Depending on the time frame of your unit of study, you could give pupils a selection of decades, years, months or even specific dates. Once they have chosen six dates for their bingo card from your selection, you could describe an event or two that happened at that time, and from this they have to work out if they have that date on their card. If so, they cross it off, until all six of their choices are crossed off and they call out 'bingo'.

You can make this more of a challenge by asking the winner to tell you what event it was that happened on each date on their card, or to expand upon one of the events.

KEY DATES BINGO

SPEECH BUBBLES

This activity requires some minimal preparation. Choose a painting, portrait or textbook picture from one of your previous lessons. Make sure there are at least two people in the picture. Photocopy the picture and then draw large speech bubbles coming from the mouth of each character. The idea is that the pupils fill in the speech bubbles with something appropriate from the previous lesson. They may need some help the first few times you try this, so you could write a question in the first speech bubble for them to answer.

For example, if you're studying the Romans, you may have a picture of two soldiers. The first could be asking the second something simple like 'how many soldiers are in our legion?' Or you could ask something that requires a more extended response, such as 'what armour do I need to pick up from the stores?'

A picture of Henry VIII with his children could have Mary asking her siblings who their mothers were, or something more demanding like why Henry divorced her mother.

When you have prepared your picture, you could either photocopy it for pairs of pupils to fill in, or display it on a whiteboard as pupils enter the classroom. Hear some of the pupils' suggestions and use them to bridge the previous lesson with the current one.

To test the pupils' knowledge of key words, provide them with anagrams of some of the vocabulary from the previous lesson. Write four or five anagrams on the board, and ask pairs of pupils to puzzle them out. Some pupils will be able to do this very quickly, so the next stage is for them to prepare a crossword-type clue for each word. These clues can then be used to help those for whom word puzzles are not a strong point!

An example of this could be the pupils studying the Victorians who have already solved the anagrams of the words 'slums', 'suburbs', 'overcrowding', 'disease' and 'poverty'. Encourage them to think of clues to each word that would help those struggling to unscramble the letters of the anagram. For 'disease' they might just say 'cholera and TB are examples of this', or create a more sophisticated clue if they are more able.

Alternatively, you could ask the pupils to make a sentence or two containing all the words to summarize what they learned the previous lesson.

PUZZLE IT OUT

PREPARE TO DISCUSS

Pair up the pupils for the first 5 minutes of the lesson. If any pupil was absent from the previous lesson, make sure they are paired with somebody who was present. Ask them to find the five most important key points from the last lesson, and tell them to be prepared to discuss them with the class. For variety, you could ask them to present the five points in newspaper headline form or as a radio news bulletin.

Some classes may need more guidance, especially when you first use this activity, so you could give them some direction with five questions that you write up on the board, or with picture clues. If they need extra guidance, you can give them about eight picture clues or questions and ask them to pick the most important five, in their opinion. They must be prepared to defend their decisions to the rest of the group. They could also rank the five in order of importance, and be expected to defend their list when comparing it to another group's.

Not all starters necessarily reinforce key points from the previous lesson. You may need to introduce a new topic, and this activity works well if your lesson is focusing on picture sources. Give each pair a picture that you'll be studying during the lesson; the more detailed the better. If you have a whiteboard, you could show it on that. Let the pupils see the picture for one or two minutes only. When they can no longer see the picture, ask the pairs to come up with a list of details about it. They could make up questions from their notes to quiz a neighbouring pair about the picture.

To focus their attention back on the picture let them see it again, and then ask them how they think it fits into what they've been studying. If it's a new topic, they can start to play detective with your guidance. Depending on the picture, ask questions to get them thinking about whether it's a primary or secondary source, what type of people are in the picture, what activities are going on, whether there are clues to the historical period, and so on.

An alternative to this is to make jigsaws from the pictures. This is useful if you want them to really focus on the detail of the pictures. You could leave one piece out and ask them to imagine what goes in the space.

If you laminate pictures before handing them out, they can be used again. Laminated pictures can also be drawn on with board pens, so the pupils can circle significant things or write the answers to questions you ask them.

PICTURE PERFECT

THE GOOD, THE BAD AND THE UGLY

This starter requires some preparation. Divide the class into two halves, but only for your benefit – don't tell them that there are any differences yet! Give individuals or pairs on one side of the class one set of sources about a person or event. Give those in the other half a contradictory set of sources. For example, if you are studying the Spanish Armada, give the first half sources that show victory was a result of good planning, and the other half sources that show victory was merely luck. You may find that topics like this one allow you to have three different viewpoints.

Where possible, you can use picture sources too, as well as newspaper headlines, depending on your topic. Ask the individuals or pairs to write a short summary of the sources, or list the points that they make. Then ask for feedback, first from one side, then from the other. This is always an amusing one to watch, as their faces can be a picture when they hear what the pupils on the other side have to say! It's a really useful way of showing how sources can differ.

JEOPARDY

Based on the game show of the same name, this involves giving the answer to the class, who then have to formulate the question. For example, tell them 'motte and bailey' and the question could be 'what were the earliest types of castle?' Or '1914' could be the answer for 'when did the Great War start?' To involve everybody, the person who gets the right question could then give an answer to somebody of their choice who hasn't yet played, until everybody has had a turn.

You can have lots of fun using a points system and time penalties, and even have a league going each term. Other ways of involving every pupil is to pass the answers and questions around the class in seat order or register order. If you want to quieten down a noisy class, they could do this as a written activity instead.

It can also be used if you have pupils turning up to your lesson at different times. Have a series of answers written up on the board, along with a clear aim such as having at least five questions formulated by a certain time. Pupils can then get on with the task as soon as they arrive.

REPETITION AND
REINFORCEMENT ACTIVITIES

Shorter starter activities can be used to reinforce points during a lesson, or motivate pupils if they are suffering from 'Friday afternoon' syndrome. Here are some that can be used as starter activities or otherwise during a lesson.

Outlaw. This starter can be done as a class or in smaller groups. Choose a pupil to be the describer and give them a key word or event. They have to describe this without using the outlawed word or phrase.

Wordsearch. Create a topical wordsearch by hand or use one of the puzzle makers on the Internet. To make it more difficult, don't tell the pupils the words they are looking for. Put a time limit on completing the wordsearch. Looking for key vocabulary will help them to learn spellings and remember key words.

Twenty questions. Pick a key person or event that you're currently studying. Tell the pupils they have 20 chances to work out who or what you are, but you can only answer 'yes' or 'no' to their questions.

Hangman. Another old favourite, this game helps pupils recall key vocabulary or phrases. One pupil draws the dashes for each letter on the board, and you can go round the class asking for letters, or leave the pupil at the front to choose from those with their hands up. Get poor spellers to check their word with you first! For a twist to the game, ask the pupil who is going to guess the word to put it into a sentence, or ask the whole class to write down five associated words or phrases to go with the answer once it's revealed.

Odd one out. Show the pupils four words, objects or pictures, one of which doesn't fit with the rest. Ask them to choose the odd one out and explain why. Then ask each of them to create their own round of 'odd one out' based on what they learn today. This can then be played at the end of the lesson.

It's easy to adapt other board games or game show ideas. For example, choose a pupil to draw a picture of something important from the previous lesson on the board, and the others have to guess its significance. Games like this are a great incentive to turn up to your lessons on time, especially if you pick the pupil to do the drawing or writing from those through your door first.

STARTING A NEW TOPIC

Before you start a new topic, it pays to ask the pupils what they already know, or think they know, about the period. Gather all their prior knowledge together on the board or a large piece of paper, and if there are misconceptions you can tell the pupils that you will come back to the list at the end of the study so they can see which ideas were valid and which have been proven wrong.

To make the pupils feel more involved in their learning, once you have elicited the knowledge that the class already has, ask individuals to write down five or ten questions that they would ask the people they're about to study, if they had the chance. A popular question, especially among younger pupils, is 'where do you go to the toilet?', and this is always a good starting place for a number of investigations: health and hygiene, inventions, homes, and so on. Tell the pupils to constantly refer back to their list, and tick questions that have been covered in lessons, or write in short answers when they have found them out. Any questions not answered during the course of study could form part of a research project or become a homework challenge.

Understanding chronology

INTRODUCING TIMELINES

Timelines can be created from Key Stage 1 upwards. They help the pupils to understand the flow of time and how time is divided up. At first, timelines can simply relate to the pupils themselves, for example showing what they do in an average school day. Build it up to a week's timeline, then a timeline showing key events since they were born. Comparing pupils within a class can also show them how they can all be the same age in years, yet some of their classmates will be almost a year older than others.

The timelines can then become more complex, by introducing notions of BC and AD. Timelines can concentrate on a specific period, such as the events of Queen Victoria's reign, or on topics such as toys throughout time.

Introducing the notion of a timeline can be tricky. One way to do it is to write out a series of times or dates on pieces of paper and give them to individual pupils who hold them up at the front of the class. The rest of the class have to arrange them in chronological order. To make it easier, make the pieces into parts of a jigsaw, so that there is only one way they can fit together.

Timelines can make interesting classroom displays. At the beginning of a topic, you could fix a blank timeline to the wall, or even right around the classroom, marking out the years that will be covered. As pupils produce work and drawings, the best examples can be stuck to the appropriate places of the timeline. Homework can consist of research activities to add. Your school may even have corridor space that allows you to accommodate the work of several different year groups.

Timelines can also be achieved by using string and pegs across the ceiling of the classroom, with units of time marked out by coloured string or ribbons and key events pegged onto the line. You could even use the back of a roll of old wallpaper if you don't have the space to display a timeline permanently, or if you teach in a number of different rooms.

Finally, you can make a game of chronology! Make a series of cards with various dates on, both AD and BC, and just like the game show *Play Your Cards Right*, you reveal one card at a time and ask the class to state if it's earlier or later than the previous card.

CREATIVE TIMELINES

TERMINOLOGY

Introducing new words and concepts can spur on the most able pupils. When discussing chronology and the way we mark out time, you might like to explain that the way of measuring years in the British system is different to the methods used by other cultures.

Here's some information you can give them: the words Before Christ (BC) and Anno Domini (AD, the year of the Lord) are particular to Christianity. Sometimes they are referred to as BCE and CE: Before the Common Era and the Common Era. Muslims start their numbered years from when Mohammed moved from Mecca to Medinah, so the year 2000 AD was the Muslim year 1422 AH. The abbreviation AH refers to Al-Hijra, the years after the emigration. Judaism saw the year 2000 AD as the year 5761, numbered after the date when God created the world according to the Torah.

Finding out other numbering systems could be a way of incorporating numeracy into history, or form project work for gifted and talented pupils. They could work out the current date according to other dating systems, or investigate other ways of measuring time.

There's no getting away from the fact that families can be so complicated, with step-siblings and remarriages, that pupils can get very confused when asked to produce a family tree. Instead, start by using a fictional family that most of them will know: *The Simpsons* cartoon is popular enough even if not every pupil has seen it. You can print off some pictures of the family from the Internet, and group together those who know the cartoon with those who are not quite sure. The added bonus is that there are three generations who are visually distinguishable: three children, two parents and the mother's sisters, and two grandparents, one from each side.

The pupils can arrange the pictures in the right way first of all, then draw a family tree using the conventions that you show them, before labelling it and sticking the pictures on. Once they have grasped this, you may then feel brave enough to ask them to complete their own. Some pupils do find this a sensitive task, so it pays to have another set of fictional family pictures for them to use instead. Or if you want to show how to include divorces and remarriages, you could use the example of the royal family, whether it's the Windsors or the Tudors.

FAMILY TREES MADE EASY

For a general introduction for younger pupils, using the metaphor of a tree is a good way to show them how we depend upon the past. Find a picture of a tree that includes the roots. Anything below ground would be the civilizations of BC, and anything growing above ground will be AD. You can stick labels to your picture which are relevant to the topics you've been studying, with the pupils themselves at the very top of the tree. Hopefully they will begin to see how what happened in the past affects where we are today: if the branch carrying the Tudors label had snapped off, for example, how would that affect what happened after it?

As a starting point for enquiries concerning cause and consequence, make grids or score sheets. At the top write your focus of study, for example: 'what caused the Spanish to invade England?' Either give the pupils different reasons, or let them develop their own list from the work you've completed. Start them off by asking them to give a score out of ten for how important each reason is. Then challenge them to find evidence to support their score. From a simple activity like filling in a score out of ten, you can pursue an enquiry and even develop this into essay writing, with each of the causes being a paragraph in the essay.

Grids, tables, score sheets: however you phrase it, they have a useful role to play when you want to show change over a period of time. Your enquiry may be: 'how did steam power transform Britain?' In this case your grid needs two columns, one for 'before steam power' and one for 'after'. Either give the pupils the categories to look at, such as transport, industry, and so on, or ask them to decide on their own categories.

Enquiries may not be so specific; primary school pupils could investigate how different Britain was at the end of the Victorian period to the beginning, with different groups concentrating on one or two topics, or individuals completing project work on something they found particularly interesting.

Similar activities can be carried out with different groups representing different viewpoints. For example, if studying the Aztecs and the explorer Cortes, half the class could show the changes that the Aztecs experienced from this encounter, while the other half could focus on a different viewpoint, in this case, that of the Europeans. Or with a topic like the Victorians, pupils could look at changes such as the introduction of the railway from different angles: the coach owner, the manufacturer and the countryside dweller.

Written activities

Pieces of work in history often rely on a written outcome, and the heavy workload of writing can be off-putting to some pupils who struggle with literacy. You can add diversity to the writing activities by including some of the suggestions here in each topic. Many of them will test the same skills as regular question and answer work and require the same depth of knowledge and understanding. There are also cross-curricular links with literacy. In addition, many of the suggestions incorporate opportunities for the pupils to empathize with people in the past. Just remember, it's much easier for a child to empathize with somebody they could relate to, like another child, than with a Victorian businessman or Tudor beggar!

One word of warning: for many of these written activities suggested, there will be one bright spark who alerts you to the fact that not many people could read and write 'back then'. Either be prepared with a story about how this character happens to be literate, or come clean and use it as a chance to tell them how lucky they are that they have the opportunity to learn these things in school!

Diary entries demand empathy from the pupils, but are a good way of getting them to think from somebody else's perspective and to really imagine what it was like to live in the period they're studying.

You can ask the pupils to write the diary entry of a figure from history, such as Florence Nightingale or Isambard Kingdom Brunel. They could write as if they were present for a specific event, but remember that it's easier for younger children to write from a child's perspective, so in these cases choose a young character for them to emulate. For example, when Howard Carter discovered the tomb of Tutankhamun, it was the young boy who carried water for the workers who first discovered the location of the steps as he sat playing with a stick in the dust. Ask them to imagine that they are the boy, rather than Howard Carter.

Or you can create a scenario for them based on a historical event. They could write the diary of a child who witnessed Norman soldiers taking over their village. They could be the novice nun or monk who is told Henry VIII is going to close their abbey. Or they could be the ancient Greek boy sent away to train as a soldier.

Help out the less able with writing frames, or at least elicit from the class the key points they should include, and keep these displayed somewhere where every pupil can refer to them as they write.

LETTERS

Writing a letter can be an alternative to writing a diary entry and a chance for pupils to show they can recall and explain events, but it also has its own uses for when you want them to produce something persuasive or biased.

For example, they could write a letter to Parliament stating their support for, or opposition to, the Poor Laws. When studying World War I, pupils could write a 'letter from the trenches', first of all explaining what it was really like, and then censoring each other's letters as they would have been before being sent to relatives back home.

Younger pupils and the less able would benefit from lists of key words and writing frames to help them in tasks like this, but once they get the hang of it they can produce some lively work that's a lot more entertaining to mark than pages of questions and answers. They might also be keen to make their work look realistic: this may involve aging the paper to make it appear like a scroll (see Idea 78) or finding an authentic looking font if they are typing up their work. Just remind them that their work must be legible!

A shorter version of the letter writing task is to produce a postcard. You can stick to being historically accurate and only use this task if you're studying a topic from the nineteenth or twentieth centuries. Or you can ask the pupils to cooperate with this anachronism: perhaps a chance to discuss why there weren't postcards in Tudor times!

For the postcard task they not only have to produce the writing, but also choose or draw a picture to go on the other side. Give them pieces of card to make their postcards. If you are pushed for time, give them a set of pictures to choose from for their postcard and muddle in some pictures that don't belong to the period you're studying to test that they've grasped the chronology.

Examples of how you can use this task include: imagine you're a servant in a Victorian house and are allowed to write to your mother to tell her what it's like; imagine you've moved to a Tudor town from a village and are letting your family know what you're up to; imagine you're aboard a ship that's off to explore the unknown; or imagine you're a Roman soldier sent to Hadrian's Wall, and you want your family back in Rome to know you miss them.

POSTCARDS – CHOOSING PICTURES AND WRITING TEXT

MAKING A HISTORY BOOK FOR YOUNGER CHILDREN

This is a way for pupils to show they've understood the topic, and it's also a way to ensure they choose their own words to convey information. In this case, it can be a suitable task after research-based homework where they have to use and adapt the information they've brought to the lesson.

Tell them they have to explain what they've learned to children in a younger year group, making sure they explain difficult words or use simpler alternatives. They can include their own illustrations, or choose from a selection you provide for them. You might like to show them some examples to give them ideas, as Year 3 can seem a long time ago to a Year 8 pupil!

If you work in a secondary school, this is a good opportunity to develop links with feeder primary schools. Pupils could send their books to a primary class, or take them in to the local primary school to show them. The primary pupils could then provide feedback, saying what they learned and what they liked best about the books. Alternatively, the finished results could be scanned onto the school's website and accessed this way. This is a particularly useful project if the topic is being studied simultaneously in the primary and secondary schools, such as the Tudors, but make sure the Key Stage 3 pupils are adding to the primary children's knowledge by introducing a range of more advanced sources for them to sift through and analyse.

Another way to display information is for pupils to make their own pages for a textbook. Show them examples from your own textbooks, and ask them which features they find most useful or appealing. This work can be done on A3 paper by individuals or pairs. They could formulate their own title as a question, which will help them to keep their work relevant because you can ask them if every piece of information they are including helps to answer the question. This should stop them filling up their page with irrelevant points.

Some of the features they could include are boxes, bullet points, narrative writing, tables and graphs, timelines, suitable sources from a selection you provide, their own illustrations, a series of questions or activities for their imaginary readers to complete and glossaries or word searches of key vocabulary. If you provide pupils with contradictory and challenging sources, this fulfils the criteria for seeking out bias and analysing why different groups of people record events in different ways.

You could take this a step further by swapping the completed pages around the class and asking other pupils to critique the work and tackle their questions, perhaps before a final draft is produced. This kind of activity can be a useful wall filler if you have an open evening coming up!

DESIGNING A WEBSITE PAGE ON PAPER

This is an alternative to producing a textbook page, and if you have access to the technology it can become an ICT activity, perhaps in conjunction with the IT department. Tell the pupils who their audience is: it could be for people who know nothing of the topic, for other pupils studying the same topic or for those who already know a lot about the topic and want to find out more.

This could be project work with different groups of pupils researching an area of particular interest to them. You may have one group working on fashion and clothes of the era, another on houses and furniture, and so on. If the final result is on paper, it should appear how a webpage might appear on a screen. To give them some ideas about how webpages differ from books, print or display a variety of examples, or encourage them to find their own as a homework task. Some points to bear in mind are that successful webpages rarely include much scrolling down – instead, they make the most of links to other pages. Pupils could pick out the key words of the topic, which would be the clickable links on a website, and this could start them thinking about how the topic would connect to others that they have studied.

This is an area open for cross-curricular links, this time with food technology. However, if practical reconstructions of old recipes aren't possible, you can still investigate the eating habits of those in the past.

This is a fun activity, probably more suited as an end of term task. Compile a list of all the food stuffs available to the people of the period you've studied. You could even divide the class into groups if there are discernible differences between what the rich and poor had access to. The pupils have to create a menu for a special or ordinary meal. It could be a menu board at a market stall, or a scroll for a Tudor feast. They could develop their research skills by using the Internet to source pictures of authentic looking dishes: reconstruction groups with websites are a useful place to look, as are the websites of historic buildings and groups who have themed days. Alternatively, bring in a selection of books they can use, along with photocopies of the pictures that they can stick onto their work and colour in.

This could also be an opportunity to talk about related topics. For example, start off by discussing the food available to the rich and the poor, and then use it as a springboard to explore issues such as class or social responsibility.

FOOD FOR THOUGHT: RECIPES AND MENUS

BUILDING FOR SALE – WRITING AN ESTATE AGENT'S ADVERT

Whether it's a Norman square keep castle, Iron Age roundhouse, Roman villa or a Tudor merchant's house, studying buildings is an integral part of history. We have photos, ruins and reconstructions, and these can all be used to build a picture of what it was like to live in the past. Explain to your pupils that not all of these houses would have been bought and sold as we do today, but ask them to imagine that a sneaky sheriff, general or lord has asked them to draw up an advert to sell the building because of some dispute of your own invention.

Bring in some genuine literature from an estate agent to show them what you expect, and once you've gone through what such an advert contains, they can produce their own for the building of your study. Usually, it should contain one or more pictures of the building, a description of its rooms and special features, its location and any furniture that's included. They shouldn't worry about including a price; if they insist, they could write that it's 'up for auction' or to 'enquire within' for more details. This activity can be a more interesting alternative to copying a diagram into their books.

Major event in history makes front page! Whether you use ICT or complete this activity by hand, it's a demanding task to get the most from your pupils. Don't just expect them to know what features a newspaper has: be prepared to show them examples of real papers, and also of mocked up historical pages that abound in the children's sections of bookstores and libraries.

The most conscientious pupils will want their newspapers to look realistic, and will write in columns and include a price and possibly a banner telling readers what's inside their paper. Less able pupils will struggle to produce a piece of structured work, and will probably need writing frames to help them include all the necessary information, as well as a ready made sheet with boxes for the newspaper name, date, headline and picture.

Newspaper articles have a style different to other types of writing in that they start off with an overview of the event, and then go into further details, possibly even including interviews with eye-witnesses. You will need to explain this the first time you try this activity, possibly using models to show what you mean.

Once you've introduced the concept of bias to your class, the newspaper activity is an ideal way for them to produce a biased piece of writing. For example, reporting on the Battle of Hastings they might choose to write as a Saxon or a Norman, and you can have fun thinking up newspaper names and headlines for each side. If you're studying the Reformation, they can choose to write their article for either the Catholic Courier or the Protestant Press.

NEWSPAPER FRONT PAGE

Primary school children can start to write essays on topics by using writing frames to guide them, but more often essay writing is introduced in secondary schools. Groups can gather evidence on a topic, and then use the information to produce their own essays. It's a skill that can be developed throughout Key Stage 3, with writing frames to support pupils when they first start to write extended pieces in Year 7. It can seem formulaic at first, but only in the same way that a series of questions and answers can.

For each piece attempted, you can gradually remove the scaffolding until the pupils feel confident about producing their own structured piece of work, prompted just by questions or clues about what to include.

You can use analogies to show them what an essay should consist of: a popular one is the 'burger' analogy. Show them a picture of a burger in a bun. The top bun is the introduction to the essay, the burger is the filling and the bottom bun is the conclusion. Each part is needed to make the burger complete, but the main part is the meaty filling. You may need to think of a vegetarian alternative!

Encourage them to redraft their work and to back up the points they make by referring to the evidence, such as the sources you have studied. Then they should explain what the evidence means. This method can be neatly summed up in an acronym they will find amusing: PEE. It stands for Point, Evidence (or Example) and Explanation. Introducing essay writing by Key Stage 3 ensures they are prepared for GCSEs, whether or not they continue to study history.

If you have studied historical figures and want the pupils to show they understand the main events of their lives or their contributions to society, they can present the information as an obituary. Find some simple examples from the newspaper and demonstrate what an obituary consists of before asking them to use the model to write one about their key historical figure. This is an activity that allows pupils to evaluate sources for bias. You can also ask that they write their obituary from a biased stance if you want them to draw conclusions about whether the figure was a 'good guy' or 'bad guy'.

A shorter way to do this sort of task is to write epitaphs for the graves of the historical figures which summarize their achievements in a sentence or two. Again, if the historical figure is a controversial one, such as Oliver Cromwell, they could produce pairs of epitaphs that show the differing opinions, or they could weigh up the evidence to come to their own conclusions. The epitaphs could also be used to start a class debate on the figure and their contributions or motives.

Epitaph writing for an imaginary family tomb can help them to understand family relations if the societal set-up was different to our own.

REPORTS

When you want to encourage pupils to study sources closely and start to evaluate them, writing reports is one way to do it. Tell them they are gathering evidence for the monarch, or for the government or even for a peasants' revolt. An example of this is compiling a report on monasteries for Henry VIII, or gathering evidence for the government to decide if Richard III was a good king. The reports could be objective and balanced, or you ask them to pick out only the information that shows that the monasteries were corrupt, or that Richard was a brave soldier, as an example of using bias.

The report could be for an explorer to convince a monarch to send them on an expedition to the new world or reasons for the Emperor Hadrian to build a wall in the north of England. Once again, by asking different groups of pupils to produce reports for different purposes, or opposing reports, this work can then be a springboard for a class debate or some substantial essay work.

EXTENSION WORK

Whether your class is set, streamed or mixed ability, there will always be some pupils who whiz through the work and require extra tasks. First of all, check why the pupil has finished: they may not require extension work because it may be they've only completed the task on a very superficial level. If this is the case, they'll need to have another go at the original piece of work or be given something to consolidate the same skills, knowledge or understanding.

The more able pupils, who finish the work quickly and to a high standard, will need something to 'stretch' them. For these pupils, you can draw on materials from later key stages or higher levels of study, although this is much easier to introduce on a whole-class basis rather than to individuals within a group.

On an individual basis, some pupils may welcome extra work, but to encourage those who are reluctant to pick up their pens again after working hard to complete the task, make sure the extension work is something that will engage and motivate them. Having access to computers can help, but that's not always practical. Project work will enable pupils to carry on with a topic of their own choosing once they have completed the regular class work. You could set up an investigative project, with the emphasis on the particular skills that the pupil needs to, or is ready to, develop further.

Drama activities

When you have a lively class, the idea of them out of their seats doing drama activities can send a shudder down your spine. However, with clear rules and instructions, and lots of structure, drama activities can really benefit history lessons. They can bring the subject to life, help pupils to understand the motivations of the people they're studying and engage those with poorer literacy skills who may be put off by the amount of writing that history lessons can involve. Very often, any acting that pupils do will be the thing that sticks in their minds long after the textbooks have been put back on the shelves.

Drama activities are usually noisier than the average lesson, and so it helps to have a pre-arranged signal with the class so that they know when to be quiet. This will also save your voice! Explain to them that when you put your hand up in the air, they must raise their hand as well to show they have seen the signal and they should then stand still and be quiet. To encourage them, you could have a forfeit for the last person to raise their hand, such as collecting in the books at the end of the lesson or putting up the chairs.

Drama activities usually mean group work. To avoid the cluster of boys who want to play fight, or the quietest children being left out, place them into groups yourself. There are a number of ways you can do this: random numbering around the class, by register order, making sure each group has boys and girls, and so on.

The pupils can gain insights into the lives of people in the past, as well as incorporating their newly gained knowledge, by taking on the role of a character in a short play they make up themselves. This can either be based on a situation you give them, or on historical figures at a particular event.

For example, if you're studying the feudal system as part of medieval realms ask pupils to form into groups, with one playing the father of the family, one as the mother, one as the reeve and the rest as children. Let them decide on the kinds of jobs their character would do and then give them a situation, such as: the reeve catches one of the children stealing an apple from the lord of the manor's orchard. What happens when he turns up at the family's hut?

Some drama activities may need a bit more structure or for the pupils to have extra information about their character. In this case, you could produce cards with some basic information about their likes or dislikes, preferences, beliefs or whatever else fits into the particular situation. You may find cards like this ready for photocopying in the teacher resource material that accompanies your textbooks.

WARMING UP

Once the pupils are in role you can keep adding new situations. For the pupils playing medieval villagers, give out cards or display on the board the next situation their characters must deal with. How would they react if, at the height of the Black Death outbreak, a stranger arrives at their village and asks to be put up for the night?

Role-plays can also feature famous historical figures. Pairs of children can explain what the Great Exhibition of 1851 was like by taking on the roles of Queen Victoria and Prince Albert.

With role-plays, the idea is to improvise how their characters would react so there is no need for them to script anything. They could use resources to help them though. Acting out the stages of the 'journey to the afterlife' that the ancient Egyptians believed in is difficult without prompt sheets, but being physically involved helps the pupils remember the sequence of events.

Sometimes in drama activities you have a child who, for reasons of shyness or otherwise, refuses to take part in any acting. Create a part for them as director of their group. They have to make sure that each character has enough lines to say, is facing the audience when they speak and that the group includes all the necessary details.

This is where you, or one of the pupils, take on the role of a character from history and respond to the rest of the class's questions. The person in the hot seat has to know their topic well, and be able to stay in character, so it's probably something for the teacher to do the first few times you use it. Start the whole thing off once you've learned enough about an event or historical figure. Again, it doesn't have to be somebody famous – it could be an eye-witness who experienced the Great Fire of London, life in the trenches, Julius Caesar attempting to invade Britain or somebody who saw the first steam train. Ask your pupils to jot down one or two questions they would ask the person if they could, so that everybody has something prepared at the start. Once the activity starts, questions should become more spontaneous as each line of questioning follows its natural course.

You may wish to assign the pupils to different groups, so that their questions come from different perspectives. For example, if you're studying Oliver Cromwell, one group could represent Parliamentarians and another represent the Royalists. If you are learning about the Roman invasion of Britain, tell half the class that they are against the Romans coming to Britain, and the other half that there might be benefits if they don't oppose the invaders.

If you wanted to have a written outcome for this activity, the pupils can write up what they've learned, perhaps as an interview for the local newspaper or magazine of the time.

MAKING PLAYS

This activity is a step beyond role-play and hot-seating activities because the pupils should come up with a script that can be practised and modified. It's useful if there's a lot of information for them to remember that would be forgotten in a role-play, and also if you manage to convince them to perform their play to another class or even in assembly. Involving various characters with different viewpoints gets them analysing sources for bias as research.

There are ready made history plays available, some with a humorous slant, and others that crop up in special needs resources to help the pupils understand how and why events happened. Often these involve a trial, historical or imagined, such as the trial of King Charles I. Having pupils act out the parts instead of reading about it from a book brings the situation to life.

To extend this into project work, bring in other factors for the pupils to consider. This can be anything from drawing the costumes that the characters would be wearing, with historical accuracy, to considering whether a servant would be able to address a courtroom full of politicians.

This is another way of getting pupils to think as their characters and reach conclusions about their actions. Base this activity on the popular format of TV chat shows – it's probably best not to mention Jerry Springer unless you don't mind excessive noise and chanting! In groups, pupils should decide who's going to play the chat show host and which other characters they need.

Chat shows are a chance for each character to be interviewed about their role in a situation or event, whether they're a named historical figure like Oliver Cromwell or a representative of a point of view, such as a roundhead soldier. They also usually allow the audience to draw conclusions about who is at fault, or what could have been done differently. You can allow figures to be brought back from the dead to comment on events.

After each group shows their chat show to the rest of the class, you could have an audience vote on one of the issues it raises. Or each group could open up questions to the audience, which will keep the audience on their toes, especially if you threaten to pick one of them at random to ask the questions!

THE CHAT SHOW CHALLENGE

AVOIDING A HEADACHE WITH GROUP DRAMA WORK

If your pupils can become boisterous during drama activities, in particular with activities like the chat show, keep a firm structure on the lesson. Start by sorting them into groups and give them tight schedules to work to, for example 2 minutes to decide who is playing which character. It can help to tell them that if they don't choose by then, you'll give them each parts to play. Some of them might even prefer it if you allocate parts. One way to do this is to ask each group to number its members one to five (or however many). Write up the numbers on the board and then next to each number write a character name, so that all those with number one will be playing the servant, and all the number fives are Queen Victoria.

Before they get out of their seats to 'act', give them another 5 or 10 minutes to work on a loose script. With the chat show activity, for example, the host must have a series of questions to ask the guests, and the guests must know how their character would respond. Advise them to read through their parts once or twice so they all know what they're doing. Only when they have some structure can they start to arrange their chairs and act.

If the idea of your class out of their seats and attempting to act really does fill you with horror, there's another way to incorporate drama into your lessons. However, they need not leave their chairs if they produce a radio news broadcast.

There are several ways to do this. One is to produce a straightforward report on an event that you've studied. You could ask different groups to be radio stations in different countries, for example British, Italian and Russian broadcasts if you're studying the World Wars. This way you should end up with working examples of biased reports.

Another variable is to have your groups working on producing reports of an event, but at various points in the lesson you reveal new information that they have to incorporate. This is a newsroom simulation, where breaking news has to be analysed and selected. It works well if you're studying the events of one particular day or a short period of time, like Wat Tyler and the Peasants' Revolt or battles from Hastings to Marston Moor.

To add a twist to the newsroom simulation, slip different sources to different groups. Use sources from your textbooks or invent your own, such as an interview with an eye-witness or 'leaked' official plans. This way when each group presents their broadcast to the rest of the class, the others can try to work out what that group knew that they didn't, and whether it was an advantage or not.

PREPARING A RADIO NEWS BROADCAST

SPEECHES AND DEBATE

Speeches are another activity where pupils remain in seats and it can lead on to written work. Working either in pairs or alone, you should tell them who their character is, and give them a scenario. They could be an eye-witness at an event such as a soldier in a battle, or something more demanding, like a politician arguing for the introduction of poor laws or against slavery.

When the pupils are arguing for or against a particular point of view, you could develop this into a class debate. Give the class a motion, such as 'this house believes that Oliver Cromwell no longer deserves to be Lord Protector'. Choose a pupil to propose the motion and another to second it. You will also need a pupil to oppose it, and somebody to second the opposition. Each of these pupils should prepare a speech of about two minutes with evidence to convince the rest of the class to vote their way. You could play the role of the chairperson, or nominate a pupil, and the rest of the class should prepare questions and points of information to put to the speech makers once they have given their opening speeches.

Once the class has finished debating, the proposer and opposer should sum up why the class should vote for them. Finally, there's the vote, where pupils decide if they wish to support the motion or oppose it.

FREEZE FRAME

This can also be called making tableaux (still images). In groups, you can start off by showing pictures or photographs and ask the pupils to recreate the scene they see. When you call 'freeze' they must hold the pose. The rest of the class can then make suggestions about what they think each character is about to say, or is thinking.

To develop this, for each figure in the picture allocate two pupils: one to pose and one to say what the character is thinking.

Once the pupils have got the hang of posing as their characters, start to suggest different scenarios that they must also develop into a tableau. If they are Victorians on a train journey, what happens when the steam train enters a tunnel? If they are land girls digging for victory during World War II, what happens when they hear the air raid siren? Or what about when Thomas Becket is praying with the monks and Henry II's knights burst into Canterbury Cathedral?

A digital camera would allow you to make permanent records of the freeze frames, and the groups could then annotate their own pictures with speech bubbles.

If each group is showing their drama activity to the rest of the class, there are methods of keeping the audience focused. One of these is to tell each child to prepare a question for one of the characters they are watching, and then pick a pupil at random after each performance, which keeps them on their toes.

Another method is to make the activity competitive. Each group should be given a score by those watching on pre-determined criteria, such as whether everybody stayed in role, or to what extent their characters are believable. At the end there can be a pooling of results to discover which performance was most successful, and why. This also helps the pupils to become reflective on their own group's performance, and helps them to improve for the next time. In addition, it gives you some leverage as you threaten to subtract points from teams who have a member that talks out of turn!

If you are following up the drama work with a written activity, the audience could be taking notes as they watch each performance. Again, to ensure they are doing as you've asked, select an audience member at random after each group's show and ask them to read out their notes or add them to those on the board for all the class to use.

Using Information and Communication Technology

The government recommends that history teachers utilize ICT in their teaching, specifically:

o the Internet, CD-ROMs and email for historical enquiries;
o developing databases, for example census returns;
o sorting, editing, reorganizing and structuring information on screen;
o pupils should be able to present their findings using ICT.

Knowing when to incorporate ICT into lessons requires some judgement to avoid using ICT for the sake of it with no real gains in historical knowledge, understanding or skills. It also means you'll need to plan access to ICT equipment, and should have tried out the resources yourself before letting a class loose with them. If you plan a lesson that relies on ICT or even the humble video recorder, always make sure you have a back up plan in case the equipment fails to work.

Computers can be great motivators for some pupils, and can assist the less able and those who struggle with the demanding writing elements of history lessons. They can also be used to stretch more able pupils who can use them to carry out independent work. Even just one computer in the classroom can have its uses, particularly if it has access to the Internet: you then have a world of information at your fingertips.

CD-ROMs can be an expensive investment for a department, costing the same as several textbooks, so don't buy until you try! They do have advantages over the Internet though. First, all the information is contained in one place and you could think of them as textbooks with extra features, such as quizzes, animations, film footage, sound effects, search facilities, worksheets that can be printed out and teacher notes.

Second, with a CD-ROM you don't have to worry about the school network being unable to access the Internet at any particular moment, or the website you want being inaccessible or pupils following unsuitable or distracting links. Another advantage is that Internet connections can sometimes take time to download large files, especially if lots of pupils try to access the same information at once, whereas this is not a problem with CD-ROMs.

Make sure you have explored the contents of the CD-ROM thoroughly before using it in lessons and think how you are going to incorporate it. If there is a limited number of PCs in the room, split the class into groups, with one using the PCs at any one time, and the others carrying out an activity that doesn't require whole-class teaching. You may need to make additional worksheets for the pupils to use to navigate their way around the CD-ROM and to keep them focused on their specific enquiry, rather than be distracted by the aimless joy of clicking buttons.

CD-ROMS

GETTING THE MOST FROM A VIDEO OR DVD

Information and communications technology doesn't just refer to using computers, and there's nothing new about showing a video in a lesson. But to make the most of the viewing, ensure the pupils are focused by giving them a series of questions to answer as they go along. Multiple choice questions work best, so that they don't have to spend too long looking at their question sheet rather than the video and can just tick the right answer. Give them some time before showing the video to read through the questions so they know what to look out for.

To make doubly sure that all pupils are concentrating, make two different question sheets and give them out alternately, so that those who may be prone to daydreaming can't just copy the answers from the person next to them.

You can use the video in a critical manner, evaluating it as a source along with any others you have studied. Depending on the type of video, you could critique their historical reconstructions, analyse the choice of photos or events the producers selected, or scrutinize the costumes for historical authenticity. If you wanted to take the work further, get the pupils to suggest how they would convey the subject matter in a more interesting or simpler way. They can make storyboards to show what their own programme would look like along with notes of the details they would include. And if you have a video camera, you could even bring your own class's history programme to a TV screen!

Desktop publishing programs allow the pupils to produce professional looking pieces of work such as newspaper reports. They usually contain a variety of templates meaning that even those not so proficient at using them can have their work set out in columns with headlines and pictures. There is more information on producing newspaper reports in Idea 36.

Wordprocessing programs can also be used for this type of activity, as well as being used to produce final drafts of pieces of written work of any sort. When pupils produce something this way they can see how professional their work can appear. There are tools to assist them, which can be turned on or off as appropriate, for example spell checks. With a wordprocessing program, pictures can be drawn or imported and text cut, copied and pasted. Work can be redrafted with ease without major rewrites, which is particularly useful for less confident writers, and those who despair at the sight of their own handwriting!

Desktop publishing programs could also be used to produce anything from a poster advertising for sailors to join the navy during the Great War to a brochure for visitors to Elizabethan London. Advantages include incorporating existing picture sources, producing colourful and well-presented work and being able to correct mistakes without spoiling the work.

USING DESKTOP PUBLISHING AND WORDPROCESSING

INTRODUCING NEW SKILLS

Using desktop publishing packages and wordprocessing programs is not necessarily a quicker option than writing answers into exercise books, as some children will spend ages choosing a font they like, or locating a particular letter on the keyboard or trying to find the work they have just accidentally deleted. If you are unsure of your pupils' ICT abilities, give them a brief introduction to the keys or icons they will need in the lesson before they move to the machines.

Once at the PCs, you could give them oral instructions and make sure they all follow your steps together to get started, or if they find it difficult to listen, produce a step by step worksheet that tells them exactly how to open and save a file, change the font size, and so on. And make sure they save their work every 10 minutes: give them time prompts! Some programs allow you to set up an automatic save feature, so that work is saved by the computer at regular intervals.

If you are using the computers over a series of lessons to produce a spreadsheet or newspaper article, there's no need to bombard them with an excess of features in the first lesson. Reveal one or two more features in each consecutive lesson.

If you have some pupils who you know are already quite skilled in using a program's features, pair them with a pupil who needs showing, but tell them that they are now a sort of teacher, which means they can't do everything for the other pupil; rather, they have to explain how to do it to their partner.

The National Curriculum documentation suggests using databases in history lessons, such as those containing census returns. Census information is available on the Internet, and pupils can use the data on there to build their own records, which ties in with the need to incorporate aspects of application of number. You could use local records to complete a sample census for your area, or input details from church records, or even the local graveyard or war memorials.

Unless you have a database program specifically for schools, they can be notoriously difficult to navigate around, but luckily often you will find that a spreadsheet program will perform all the functions you need in a history lesson. Inputting data onto spreadsheets can be time-consuming, especially for slow typists and bad spellers, so you may wish to prepare spreadsheets of figures in advance for use in your lessons. Once you have a sample census, there are a number of things you can do: the information can be moved around; sorted by different features such as age; deleted, changed or added to; columns and rows can be hidden or highlighted; and the pupils can perform calculations to find out the average life span, for example.

Spreadsheets can be used in lessons whenever you have data that needs compiling, sorting or calculating. Many spreadsheet programs can also produce instant bar charts, pie charts and graphs, so that pupils inputting figures on the ages of Victorian factory workers, for example, can see a visual representation of the numbers of workers in each specified age group.

FINDING WEBSITES FOR LESSONS

There are so many websites that can be used in history lessons, but because of the nature of the medium their content, design and locations can change frequently, and so it would be a futile activity to attempt to create a list of useful websites here. Generally, the BBC's website with its enormous history section and local area information is a good place to start. You can find it at www.bbc.co.uk/history.

So how do you find them? You can keep abreast of new useful websites by reading the education press. You could also visit a website that caters for history teachers and is regularly updated with new links. One such website is School History at www.schoolhistory.co.uk. These websites are often run by teachers, and resources are shared among the people who use the site. Another way is to visit the websites of other schools, who often compile lists of links for their pupils to use. The National Trust and English Heritage have dedicated education programmes, some of which can be accessed through their websites, and local archaeology units are another source.

If you are seeking something specific, use a search engine, and add a key word such as 'school' or 'lesson' to make sure you get results aimed at the right audience. Once you start to discover useful websites, bookmark them so you don't have to search for them all over again.

Websites can vary enormously in quality, as anyone can write and publish a website. Some may contain a wealth of useful information but it may be presented in a way that is hard to read on screen, or be accompanied by irritating animations or music that will distract your class. Decide if you need additional equipment, such as speakers or headphones.

Some websites may look as if they've been very professionally produced, but once you start to scrutinize the information you realize that its only use is a lesson in what not to include in an essay! The Internet is an interactive medium, and many websites make the most of this by containing online quizzes and games with instant feedback, or pictures that can be dragged and dropped into the right sections.

Once you've found a website that will be of use in your lesson, make sure you look carefully at all the pages you're going to use. No matter how good your school's firewall is, a few unsuitable websites can always appear; it's amazing what results can be returned if you search for websites on chainmail clothing, for example! If the pupils are going to need access to the website themselves, make sure they have the user privileges to do so before you try it out in the lesson.

Once you've found and analysed your website for the lesson, all you have to worry about is how you're going to use it with your class. Do you want the pupils to research information? Make sure you give them specific addresses to input to get to the right page, and give them a list of questions based on the contents to help them focus. Ban any printing or you may find their research consists of printed out pages that haven't been read, and printing straight from websites can be very wasteful. Instead, if they want print-outs of pictures or tables of information, these can be highlighted, copied and pasted into a wordprocessing document.

Some websites, such as School History (www.schoolhistory.co.uk), have interactive quizzes that can be played online to test pupils' knowledge. Pupils can use individual computers to do this, or you could show the screen on a whiteboard and make it a whole-class activity. The BBC (www.bbc.co.uk/history) has an extensive range of history webpages, some specifically for schools. There are animations and simulations, for example showing how steam engines work, and again this can be suitable to show the whole class at once on a whiteboard. Websites are developing at a phenomenal rate, and may include movie clips, sound files and animations that will enliven your lessons. Just make sure that the computer(s) you use have the right software to display all the components.

Most museums now have a presence on the Internet, and these vary from websites with very basic information to huge sites with interactive exercises and collections available to view from your own computer. These are no substitute for a real museum visit as, for example, pupils can get no real sense of scale of the objects on a screen. However, if there is no chance for a museum visit, or even if you wish to complete some work that follows on from a visit, these websites can be very useful.

Pupils could select the pictures of objects from a museum's website and rearrange them into their own gallery design to best illustrate a particular period or theme by copying and pasting the pictures into a word-processing document. Do check that you're not breaking any copyright laws before you carry out a task like this: most websites have a section telling you how you are able to use their images. Or you could set pupils some detective work, giving them descriptions of artefacts and asking them to track them down on the website by finding the right periods or exhibitions. Art gallery websites can also be used in this way.

MUSEUMS ONLINE

THE USES OF POWERPOINT

PowerPoint can be a useful program to use in history lessons, whether it's a ready made presentation that you download from the Internet and show to your class, or it's a series of slides that you prepare for the pupils to put in the right sequence, or it's an activity you create where the pupils make their own slides and use them to present a topic to the rest of the class.

PowerPoint allows users to create a series of slides which can then be shown as a slide show. Each slide can have text, pictures, sound effects, imported sound clips and even movie clips, but the first two will suffice for most pupils who are creating a presentation. Slides can be rearranged in any order so this is another way to enable pupils to attempt sequencing activities. Prepare a number of slides on a series of events or a collection of causes and effects, and then ask the pupils to arrange the slides into the correct order.

Another way to use this program in a presentation is to have the computer screen or whiteboard in a place only visible to the presenters, so that they are able to use their slides as prompts for a speech. However, giving the whole class something to focus on, such as a picture source, is more interesting for the audience and less embarrassing for nervous speakers!

The Internet really has revolutionized a lot of practices in teaching, and one that's often overlooked is the way it allows teachers to communicate with each other, sharing ideas, resources and good practice. Here are some of the resources available for teachers on the Internet:

○ There are official government websites with examples of the National Curriculum in practice.
○ There are websites created by teachers that feature webpages they've made themselves and which can be used in your lessons.
○ There are resource banks of worksheets that teachers have contributed which can be printed off and used in your lessons.
○ There are bulletin boards where you can submit questions for communities of other teachers to answer, or point you in the right direction. You can contribute your own knowledge and lesson ideas, in the spirit of sharing that has sprung up. You can even end up making contacts in other schools who would never have crossed your path without the Internet, sharing everything from inspection experiences to news of vacancies and conferences.
○ There is the wealth of information out there that can help you fill gaps in your own subject knowledge, or find resources to help answer any awkward questions you may be asked during a lesson! Need a picture of a Tudor feast or Greek armour, but the library is shut? Somewhere on the Internet you will find several examples to choose from, using a search engine or your valuable collection of links.

Using primary sources

ARTEFACTS

Artefacts can be loaned from your local education authority or museums, or you may have accumulated a collection in your department. There are companies who specialize in making replicas and they usually advertise in the education press. If you want to look at more objects from the past, many museum collections are now available to view online.

Pupils like handling objects they may have only seen in books, especially if they're unusual and they have to deduce what the object actually is.

One way to incorporate artefacts into a lesson is to tell the pupils to imagine they are curators of the class collection. Your class museum is holding an exhibition on the theme of the topic you're studying. Out of the artefacts available, which could also include those photographed in books, pupils have to choose three or four to represent the topic.

Once they've chosen their objects, they must produce a museum guide. This can be a leaflet or pamphlet or even a webpage. In the guide, they should describe the object, speculate on its uses, and state what it represents as well as what else it can tell us about the period. They could invent feasible details, such as when and where it was found. They can try their hand at illustrating it too. Further work on this may include summarizing the information for labels for each artefact, and choosing one overall design for a poster about the class's exhibition. Pupils have to justify why the object of their choice can represent the topic or theme.

Textbooks should contain a variety of primary sources for your class to examine. Textbook authors do the hard work of hunting down sources and evidence and compiling them into units of work, but gather together a selection on any one topic and you'll see how much they can vary. Choosing a textbook to use is often a matter of personal preference or practicality – that is, what your school already owns. That's not to say you can't gather your own sets of resources too.

Look out for old newspapers; sometimes national papers will reprint copies of their historical issues to mark an event like VE Day, or local papers can contain a wealth of information on what they featured this week 50 years ago. Local papers are a useful source of old photos and maps of the area: you can cut them out and stick them on cards, and they often don't lose anything by being photocopied because they're black and white anyway. You can find old photos and postcards at local car boot sales, fayres and jumble sales. Use them for exercises showing change and continuity, local history studies, displays, chronology exercises and project work on everything from architecture to fashions.

A visit to an art gallery should include a stop in the gift shop too, because you'll be able to pick up copies of the portraits and paintings in postcard or poster form. If you're keen to develop your departmental resources, you could even start to build up an oral history collection by setting the pupils a homework task of interviewing family members about a twentieth-century topic that you're studying.

OTHER PRIMARY SOURCES

Why try to explain what it was like to wear clothing from the past, when you could demonstrate with real examples? Dressing up in period costume is not only a fun activity that the pupils will remember for a long time, but it also brings a practical understanding to history. Many education departments at museums and historic buildings have sets of clothes that volunteers can be dressed in, and visits to places like castles may provide children with the opportunity to wield swords and shields (preferably of the non-lethal kind!) or try on helmets. If you invite a historical re-enactor into your school, he or she may well have clothing for the pupils to try on.

Once you have your willing volunteers trussed or corseted, encourage the other pupils to ask them questions or ask them to carry out tasks as simple as bending down or spotting an attacker approaching from behind. They will be able to work out for themselves (though hopefully not experience!) why Victorian ladies would often faint, or why some soldiers on the battlefield were at a particular disadvantage. Take photos for a display and label them. You can then follow up any kind of dressing up activity with further work in the classroom, whether it's looking at the differences in fashions between the rich and the poor, or discovering where the materials came from. With clothing from the last 500 years, look at portraits or photographs and try to identify any items they've seen or handled.

Here's a way of showing how historians come to different interpretations when working with the same sources. Read the class a short version of an event. For example, if you're studying the Romans it could be the story of how Romulus and Remus founded Rome. The two boys were taken in by a shepherd and his wife after they were found abandoned on the river bank, so ask the pupils to write the story from the point of view of either the shepherd or his wife. Tell them they can only include what the shepherd or his wife would have known from their own experiences.

They can then read out their accounts, and the rest of the class can fill in a chart of what the reader has included from the original telling of the story, and what new details they have added to make the story make sense. Use the findings to explain that this is similar to how historians work: adding their own interpretations to the primary sources they have to hand.

You could carry out this exercise by substituting a small collection of artefacts in place of a story outline. If you're studying World War II, show the pupils a bag with a name tag, along with such objects as a gas mask, a teddy bear, a ration book and a train ticket. If you don't have the actual objects, use large laminated pictures. Fill in a few details, and then ask the pupils to work out the rest of the story, again as an example of how there can be many different accounts of the same event.

DEMONSTRATING HOW GAPS IN NARRATIVES ARE FILLED

USING CONTEMPORANEOUS LITERATURE AND MUSIC

Playing music from the period you're studying can provide an air of authenticity to your classroom, especially if you play it in the background while the pupils produce work that requires them to empathize with the people they're studying. If your music department doesn't have the right recordings, local lending libraries often have music collections, and there are even some websites with sound files you can use, although the quality of these can leave a lot to be desired.

There's often the opportunity to include some of the literature from the time you're studying, which might strictly be the realm of the English department, but its inclusion is easily justified as another primary source. For example, Chaucer gives us invaluable insights into the medieval church and the lives of people in various professions, and there are many retellings of his tales in modern English. You can delve into Shakespeare's *Twelfth Night* if you're looking at Tudor Christmas celebrations, or set the scene for the Vikings by reading some sagas.

This concept is usually easily understood by children, especially if you use examples they can relate to. If you have time, you can use analogies of sports teams or pop bands to explain bias. Give them a choice of two teams or bands, one of which they must pick to support for the duration of the exercise. If it's a sports team, the teams are battling for the cup, but if it's bands they're aiming for number one in the charts. Let's use the example of football teams. You can use real examples from your locality, or invent teams; in this case: Sandbourne in the blue and Casterbridge in the red. Once they've picked their team to support, tell them that they're at the match, preparing to write a report for the club paper.

Give them an account of the match, and at points ask them to jot down a word or phrase that puts their team in a positive light, despite what happens. For example, tell them that Sandbourne won the toss at the start of the match. Was 'Sandbourne at an advantage through sheer luck' or were 'Casterbridge outclassed even before the match started'? For low ability pupils, give them pairs of phrases to choose from. Other events in the fictional match could be an own goal, a dubious penalty awarded, a player sent off and a fight on the pitch. Once they have a collection of phrases to describe each event, ask each pupil to write a paragraph on the match, showing favour to the team they chose, whether they won or lost. What they produce is a biased report, which they can compare.

EXPLAINING BIAS USING ANALOGY

EXPLAINING BIAS USING HISTORICAL EXAMPLES

If you're pressed for time in lessons, but still need to introduce the concept of bias with some obvious examples, you can prepare pairs of newspaper style headlines about the event or figure you're studying. For example, if it's the Battle of Hastings you might have 'Cheating Normans take the country by trickery' and 'Clever Normans use cunning to outwit slow Saxons'. Pupils can sort the headlines into those that support the Normans and those that support the Saxons, and then pick out the words that are biased, before having a go at making their own headlines. You can then move on to some less obvious examples using sources.

You could explain that the word 'bias' comes from a French word that means 'slanting' or one-sided. Using exercises such as those suggested here will help pupils to identify bias, but you should also explain why this is important in history. You can show them how historians create balanced accounts by finding sources of various degrees of bias one way or the other. You can demonstrate this by giving the pupils two biased sources, preferably that stand in opposition, and asking them to extract the most likely facts by finding things that both sources mention.

You may need to support work on bias with some exercises in working out how facts and opinions differ: picking the facts and opinions out of a text, for example, or asking pupils to make up three facts and three opinions for the others to sort out.

This can follow on from the previous exercise on bias.
Explain that propaganda is information given out by one
side to win support. One side will show itself to be right
and good and show the other to be wrong and possibly
evil. As such, it's biased. If they've completed the exercise
on writing biased accounts of a football match, give them
some news flashes, for example it's discovered that the
referee's brother plays for Sandbourne, or that
Casterbridge bribed the linesmen. Selecting information
from all that you give them, they must discredit the other
team while not mentioning the faults of their own.

If you prefer to use historical examples, there are
plenty to choose from, but these are not always clear to
those trying to grasp the meaning of propaganda.
Instead, create some propaganda about the historical
topic you're studying. With the Battle of Hastings, ask
the pupils to create a poster asking for soldiers to fight
on one side or the other. If they choose to support the
Normans, for example, much can be made of the broken
oaths that would have guaranteed the throne for William
of Normandy. If they're supporting the Saxons, challenge
them to find a reason why the Normans should be
discredited.

EXPLAINING SATIRE

Once pupils have grasped what satire is, they might offer to tell you a few more colloquial phrases that help them to understand the concept a bit better, and you might just wonder why you never put it like that in the first place! Satire is a form of writing, or drawing in the case of cartoons, that depicts the failings of individuals, societies or ideas as ridiculous or derisive.

You could introduce the idea by playing 'spot the difference' with a picture of a person and their caricature, either using a historical example or one of the contemporary examples you often find in newspapers. Ask the pupils why they think the person's features have been exaggerated and whether this compliments them or not. If your school encourages cross-curricular links, you may find that the discussion leads on to topics such as bullying. There are also links with work on metaphor in English.

When pupils encounter a term like satire for the first time, ask them to work on their own definition of the word to write in their exercise books for reference. This is more beneficial than copying a definition from a book, because it means you can check their understanding. Give them access to the various ways they can use the term too, introducing them to its variations, such as 'satirical'.

Being creative

Primary school history seems like the ideal opportunity to work in a cross-curricular way, combining history themes with the literacy hour, art lessons, design and technology, ICT, and so on. But the secondary school history curriculum also encourages cross-curricular links, and positively encourages the incorporation of key skills such as literacy and numeracy.

When you want to be creative in history, it helps to have some resources. For those keen on recycling, this is a good way to do it! Start saving everything from cereal boxes to ice cream tubs, and envisage their future transformations into medieval churches and ancient Greek market places.

Creative work makes history accessible to pupils who learn by more practical methods, and those who struggle with vast amounts of writing. However, pupils of all abilities usually relish the chance to do something a bit different. Some of these ideas may be more suitable for extra-curricular activities such as a history club, and many of them will provide colourful work to display on classroom walls and for open evenings.

THEMED DAY

You might be lucky enough to be able to organize a themed afternoon or day, where other departments work on a history theme. It requires a lot of planning and some timetable shuffling, and of course the cooperation of your colleagues!

If you're studying the Romans, maths departments could do work with Roman numerals or working out areas of villas or towns from plans, or take the pupils outside to show how triangulation helps archaeologists plot archaeological remains. The art department could choose from many options, such as mosaic making, sculpture or the history of art and architecture. In design and technology, the pupils can get advice about designing under floor heating in villas or efficient aqueducts. Geography lessons are ideal for showing the spread of the Roman empire, and why areas were of value to the Romans. English lessons could concentrate on mythology, stories or writings from the period or myriad ideas for creative writing. Even music lessons, PE, cookery and RE can become involved. Modern foreign languages might be willing to look at language origins with some basic Latin, and drama lessons could be an opportunity to look at Roman plays or the theatre. The issues raised by studying the Romans, such as culture, class and society, fit in well with citizenship. ICT devotees can create a website showing what happened when the Romans took over the school, or it could be reported in the school magazine.

These cross-curricular ideas are easily translated to other historical periods, such as the ancient Egyptians, Aztecs, Anglo-Saxons and Vikings, ancient Greeks, Tudors or Victorians. In fact, you may need longer than just one day once ideas start forming!

Creative activities don't have to involve lots of
preparation; in fact they can lead on from other tasks
within the lesson. Sequencing activities are useful
because pupils can show they understand chronology
and also prioritize information.

To test chronology, take your sources or pictures and
stick each onto a piece of card. Put each set into an
envelope which can be given to each pupil or group. If
you laminate each set you'll be able to use them again.
The cards can be spread out on desks and rearranged
into the right order. If they're laminated, they can be
written on with board pens and wiped clean afterwards,
allowing pupils to add notes.

Once pupils are used to these sequencing activities,
they can start to create their own which could then be
swapped around the class. For example, they could make
a series of cards showing events leading up to a war, or
how the plague reached Britain. They could create a
'pairs' matching game of reasons why the contenders to
the throne in 1066 should be king, or why the Roman
empire came to an end. They could also try matching
pictures to descriptions, for example the illustrations of
the Anglo-Saxon year to descriptions of what happened
in each month.

CARD TRICKS 1: SEQUENCING ACTIVITIES

You don't just have to stick to chronology exercises to include sequencing activities in your lessons. Pupils can prioritize reasons and causes by rearranging cards with the reasons written on them. The advantage of using cards over writing the reasons as a list straight into their books is that individuals within a group can argue their case and the list can be debated before being finalized, with cards physically rearranged. To make it more of a challenge, you can present each card with crucial words missing, also known as a cloze exercise. Another variation is to sort reasons into short-term and long-term consequences. Cards can also be arranged into political, social, religious and economic reasons, or other categories of your choosing.

Having information on cards can be used to match up pairs of causes and consequences, such as why there were so many poor people in the sixteenth century, and to encourage pupils to think of causal links between events. Having the cards in front of them will help them to create a flow diagram in their books.

CARD TRICKS 2: REARRANGING REASONS

MAKING KEY VOCABULARY ACCESSIBLE

Like many other subjects, history can sometimes seem to have a language all of its own. Encourage pupils to question words they don't understand, and dedicate the back or middle of their exercise books to building a glossary of history words so that not only do they have the meaning at their fingertips, but also the correct spellings. As mentioned in Section 2, exercises such as word searches and key vocabulary bingo will help to reinforce the spellings, while there are many starter activities to test that the pupils understand the meanings of these new words.

Display the vocabulary around the classroom too. You might choose to have the key words as labels on a diagram, so that their meanings are clear as well as their spellings. You could choose a different pupil each lesson to be the chronicler, whose job it is to provide a large copy of the correctly spelled new word for display on the wall. It's been suggested that the action of looking upwards corresponds to the part of the brain associated with memory. Try out this theory in your classroom by displaying key words in a place where children have to raise their eyes to look at it.

If the pupils have been writing a newspaper article or obituary, they may like to make it look old and faded. It's probably best not to do with a class full of children watching, but you can burn the edge of paper to make dark jagged edges that resemble an old treasure map. For the more health and safety conscious, the same effect can be achieved by rubbing a brown crayon around the edge of the paper and tearing corners off.

Cold used teabags can be dabbed onto paper to produce a sepia colour, or the paper can be slightly grilled. It's not advisable to use coffee instead of tea, as the smell lingers for a very long time! A safer alternative to genuine wax seals is to use Blu-tack or plasticine, into which pupils can carve their names or designs with a toothpick. If you want to use their documents as display work, play along with the attempts at authenticity by introducing the work as 'scrolls discovered by Year 6' or something similar.

MAKING 'DOCUMENTS' LOOK OLD

MAKING MODELS

Making models is a fun way to help children visualize what they may only have seen on a flat textbook page or computer screen. Many primary age books contain activities, such as templates, that enable children to make everything from model castles to replica pyramids and brooches. Photocopy the templates onto card. You can treat the finished pieces as artefacts for your classroom museum, or if they're stable enough you could save them to become buried 'treasure' if you run a mock excavation.

Finished artefacts could become the basis for story writing based on supporting evidence. For example, a Celtic brooch could be the souvenir that a Roman soldier takes back to show his children after a failed attempt to invade Britain. A model of a particular design of castle could be used to persuade the king that building these will provide strategic advantages over the old design.

Making models is another way of including key skills in your lessons, especially if the activity involves lots of measuring and calculating of the resources needed. If you're making model pyramids, get the children to calculate how many blocks would be needed for the real thing, and how heavy they would be, and so on.

The pupils can have a go at making a calendar when you have a point to get across about the seasons, differences in dates or annual activities. They can either make a calendar by hand, or use an ICT application with a template to fill in.

For example, if you're studying the medieval village, you might provide the pupils with a list of agricultural activities that were carried out at certain times of the year. Ask the pupils to stick the names or pictures of the activities to the correct time of year.

You could also use the calendar activity to show the differences in seasons in other parts of the world, for example if you're studying ancient Egypt. Pupils can mark off when the Egyptians expected the Nile to flood and find out the consequences of this event. A calendar could also be filled in to show the events of a specific year, for example 1066. By filling in the details about the Battles of Stamford Bridge and Hastings, pupils can visualize how long it took the Saxon army to march south, before thinking of the effects this would have on the army.

Studying the Romans or Vikings, with their different names for days of the week and months, could lead to pupils producing a calendar where each day of the week or month is illustrated with a picture of the reason why it's so named: for example, a Roman calendar could feature a picture and summary of the god Mars instead of our month of March, or a Viking calendar could explain how Thursday was so named.

MAKING A CALENDAR

1 Create a catalogue

Where there are opportunities, you can indulge in some cross-curricular links between art and history. If you've been looking at a theme such as toys or fashions, pupils can create a catalogue by drawing examples they've seen and listing their features.

2 How they used to write

Trying out handwriting or methods of writing can be a challenge. You will need equipment, such as slates or quills, if you want to try writing as Victorian schoolchildren did. After looking at medieval manuscripts such as the Lindisfarne Gospels, pupils can try decorating the initial letter of their names in similar styles. Similarly, they can try emulating some of the geometric tiles from studying Islamic civilizations, where there are also links to numeracy if you discuss the symmetry of the patterns. Civilizations with different alphabets, such as runes or hieroglyphs, provide an opportunity to make up codes or secret messages to decipher.

3 Grave concerns

When studying the Romans, there are usually lots of examples of funerary architecture. Pupils could draw gravestones containing information about characters they read about in sources as an alternative to a written exercise, such as obituary writing.

4 The art of the past

When studying the ancient Greeks, Romans and Egyptians, the class can try designing their own statues of the gods and goddesses. The Tudors provide a chance to study portraits, especially those painted to portray Queen Elizabeth in a certain manner. Pupils could have a go at painting portraits using symbolism, perhaps of other famous figures.

1 Town planning

Pupils can design or plan a village or town, including the features you insist they must include. For example, medieval villages are usually presented as having the church, common land, open fields, manor house, and so on. Looking at examples, ask the pupils to compile a list of what they would expect to find in a medieval village and then they can plan their own village, perhaps even making a model. To show change over a period, overlay their pictures with acetate and ask the pupils to draw or mark out the differences.

2 Cartoon strips

Cartoon strips or storyboards could claim the Bayeux Tapestry as an early example, and pupils can produce their own to show a series of events. If you have some reluctant artists, provide them with a selection of pictures they can choose from, and encourage them to complete the writing in each box to tell the reader what's going on.

3 Imitating past styles

Pupils can design their own heraldic shields or ancient coins featuring the heads and symbols of the appropriate leaders. There is often a cross-curricular link with RE, as the importance of religion is included in many history topics. Combine the issues by making replica stained glass windows using tissue paper, with the windows showing an important event or sequence of events.

4 Evidence and imagination

If a piece of literature ties in with your topic, such as *Beowulf* and the Anglo-Saxons, you could read the class an extract from a modern translation. Then ask them to draw what they imagine the monster to look like. You can do a similar task if you're studying Tudor

MORE ART AND HISTORY LINKS

explorers. Some of the explorers told of strange creatures they saw overseas, but when artists tried to draw the beasts from the descriptions, they came up with some very strange interpretations of animals we suppose are giraffes and elephants. Read the descriptions to the class and ask them to draw what they are told, then use the results as a practical example about interpreting sources.

History games

Archaeology fascinates many children, thanks to popular TV programmes, films and even computer games. But the emphasis in these is often on finding artefacts – raiding tombs – rather than showing people how important context can be. The object itself can only tell us so much; where it was found needs to be taken into consideration too. If you want to give your class an introduction to excavation you can play the dustbin game. This is also a useful way of introducing units of work on prehistoric periods to explain how we know about the past when there is no written record.

You will need either a real dustbin, or more likely, a large diagram of one. Fill it with household rubbish, or if you're using a diagram, you can stick on packaging and pictures of other rubbish.

You can use your dustbin to explain stratigraphy: the layers of earth you can see in cross-sections. For example, you could ask which rubbish is the oldest, and tell them that the rubbish is collected on a Monday, so what would be the date of the bottom layer of rubbish?

Get the pupils to work out which rubbish would rot the quickest. Pretend the owners of the dustbin have never heard of recycling and include a huge variety of rubbish, from plastic packaging to food scraps, from bottles and cans to newspapers. Ask them what would be left if an archaeologist found the dustbin in a year, or ten years or 100 years. Pose questions such as: 'if the label from a tin rotted away, how could we tell what had been in the tin?' What would the presence of maggots tell us?

You can also use your model dustbin to explain interpretation. What could we learn about the owners of the dustbin from the rubbish? Who lives in the household: adults, children, pets? Why might the rubbish give us a warped picture of the family? What kinds of things wouldn't they throw away in a dustbin?

You can tie this activity in with the period you're studying. People in the past may not have had dustbins, but there would have been rubbish pits or drop zones. Prepare a picture of a rubbish pit or dustbin from the period you're studying. If you're studying change over a period, include objects from the beginning of the period at the bottom and more recent objects at the top. Ask the pupils to analyse the pictures, finding out what kind of people these were from their rubbish. What kinds of objects would the people have kept rather than throw away? You can make it more of a puzzle by only including parts of objects, as if they're broken. Or you could ask the pupils to produce their own 'dustbins' of objects to show change over the period or to represent a particular person or group of people.

DUSTBIN GAME: INTERPRETATION

MAKING BOARD GAMES

An end of term or end of unit treat could be to make a board game about the topic studied. This is a good way to test knowledge and understanding. Making a board game should include compiling a series of questions, so that the pupils are selecting information, and they should also include the answers, whether these are on the back of question cards or on a separate sheet. These games can be as simple as drawing a grid on a piece of card for players to move around, or the pupils can be allowed a free rein on creativity; for example, if you've just studied the ancient Egyptians they could construct model pyramids for players to race to, or a representation of the River Nile with counters shaped as feluccas.

This activity can be adapted to whatever period you're studying. It could even be about a particular topic within a period. The theme might be based on the medieval village, with players assuming the roles of peasants who have to work their way around a board depicting a plan of the village, complete with cotton wool sheep, where the aim is to gather loaves of bread by answering questions correctly. If you've just studied the Civil War, they could create games for two teams, where an advance on the battlefield is made each time a team answers a question successfully.

Once the groups have made their games, set them out around the classroom and let each group try out the other groups' games. Ask them to grade each game they play on whether the history included is accurate, whether it's too easy or too hard as well as the presentation of the game and its playability. You could compile their results at the end to come up with a winning game.

The word 'quiz' is far less intimidating than 'test', and if you want to test knowledge and understanding, quizzes are a good way to do this. Quizzes can help the pupils with revision if they have exams coming up. Many of the activities mentioned in Section 2 can be adapted into quizzes as well as other popular formats, such as a variation on *Who Wants to be a Millionaire?*

Even better is to encourage the pupils to prepare the questions for you! After reading a section of text ask pairs or groups of pupils to make up a number of quiz questions based on what they've just read. After all the reading and question making is completed, collect in their sheets of questions and select questions from all the different groups to ask the class, either as individuals or as small groups. Winners, or even the first correct answer, can be rewarded with the incentive of leaving first when the bell rings. This type of activity ensures that the pupils absorb the information they have read and can recall it.

Team rivalry can be a great incentive to do well. If the teams are too large, however, you may find that only one or two pupils are actually doing the work. Incorporate rounds where every team member has to participate, for example a drawing round, where everybody has to produce a drawing of something you specify, whether it's a diagram of a roundhouse or a scene from the Bayeux Tapestry, before the team chooses their best example to hand to you for marking.

Out and about

INCORPORATING LOCAL HISTORY

Sometimes it's possible to take your class to see an archaeological excavation in progress. A local history society, archaeology unit or university department may run a dig that encourages visitors, and sometimes even participants. National Archaeology Day, in July each year, is an opportunity to get involved in activities in the locality, such as small-scale excavations and games.

Don't expect to spend the afternoon watching your pupils emptying wheelbarrows and shovelling piles of earth; it's more likely that they'll be able to watch finds being washed, sorted and labelled, and maybe have a go at sieving the soil from the spoil heap to see what might have been overlooked.

Local history can mean just getting out of the classroom for half an hour to look at buildings or statues nearby. You will still need to carry out a risk assessment and ask for parents' permission to take the children out of the classroom, but going to survey local architecture is free and requires minimal preparation. Some of the pupils may walk past the same buildings every day, so create a way to open up their eyes to what you really want them to see. Ask them to draw a feature such as a window or statue, or give them a multiple choice questionnaire that they can fill in just by ticking the right answer.

If you can't take the pupils out to see the history in the vicinity, bring the history into the classroom. Take a series of photos of local historical features that the pupils will recognize and produce large copies for them to study. With photos, you can zoom in on the significant features, and pupils can have a go at putting the buildings or features into chronological order, or matching the correct window to particular buildings. If you use a digital camera, you can project the images onto a whiteboard and zoom in or highlight the features you want them to focus on.

If there's a feature close to the school that pupils have access to outside of school hours, such as a war memorial, you could make the visit a homework task. Prepare a series of questions to give to each pupil and encourage them to fill in the answers as they walk home from school. Of course, this won't be practical for every pupil, so make sure you have a contingency plan for those unable to make the visit. For example, if you've asked them to note down the number of names on a war memorial, give a task based on this to the children that can't visit it, such as compiling the figures onto a spreadsheet.

Many schools are part of the area's history, and by investigating any historical features your building or grounds have, and the changes that have occurred over the years, such as new buildings or blocked up doorways, you may encourage a greater appreciation among your pupils for their environment! Aerial maps are available on the Internet, as are historical maps of local areas, and these can be used in conjunction with a local history project. Finally, get in touch with your local record office to see what they can offer schools.

Visitor centres, museums, exhibitions, heritage parks: they all clamour for school visits and you can often find brochures and pamphlets in your history department and cluttering up your pigeon-holes. Many, if not most, have worksheets or programmes for different aged children, and lots of places have education staff on hand to take your group on a tour or provide a dressing up session or on-site talk.

If you're taking a class on a visit, try to get there yourself first. Check that the exhibitions are suitable for your class and also the practicalities, like finding out where they can eat their lunches if it's raining, and where the toilets and meeting places are. You may have pupils with special needs, and your introductory visit will help you to plan for their needs too. Many of the places that encourage schools to visit will let the teacher have an introductory visit for free, so get in touch and find out what they can offer you.

Some places, especially museums, run in-service training for teachers so that they can see how beneficial a trip to that site would be, but these are also useful in showing you how to include the visit in further work you carry out at school. Some will even provide you with a ready made risk assessment for your visit. English Heritage can tailor visits to historic buildings to include cross-curricular themes, for example citizenship, and produce a teacher's guide to help you plan your visit.

If you're studying the history of the twentieth century, you may have a willing grandparent who can come into school and share their experiences and memorabilia with the pupils. Some local museums offer a service where their education officer will come in and give a talk, bringing objects for the children to handle as well. Often there's a small fee per child, but it can be less hassle and less time consuming than bussing the pupils to the museum to see something specific. Other experts may have specific skills to show your class, such as spinning and weaving or flint-knapping. Your local museum should be able to suggest contacts for this type of visitor.

Re-enactors can also be invited into schools, along with their artefacts and costumes. Ask around the schools in your area to find out if there are any recommendations for local re-enactors, or look out for advertisements in the education press. Many charge travel expenses on top of a one-off fee and/or a fee per child. Re-enactors are enthusiasts about their particular period and accumulate a large collection of objects and authentic looking costumes. Some of them are ex-teachers or actors, and a surprising amount of them have a good working knowledge of the National Curriculum and will tailor their visit to your requirements. However, a word of advice from personal experience: remember to warn the rest of the school if your re-enactor intends to perform a demonstration using gunpowder!

Plenary activities and homework

Lots of the starter activities can be adapted to use at the end of the lesson, with the added incentive that the group or table with the best answers can leave the lesson first (which works especially well if your lesson is before a break!).

When setting homework tasks, you should do it before your lesson plenary. Sometimes, much of the lesson is working towards a homework task, so explain the homework near the beginning, and keep referring back to it throughout the lesson. Pupils should be selecting information and ideas that they can use for their task.

When you set homework, ask yourself why you're setting it. It shouldn't just be an afterthought to the lesson, something you set because homework is timetabled for that day. Homework is a chance for the pupils to show how much they've learned and understood when they don't have the support of their teacher around. It's a chance for you to check that they've been paying attention! But homework can also be an opportunity to prepare for a future lesson by carrying out research or to work on projects.

Test the pupils' knowledge and understanding from the lesson in a number of ways. Ask them quiz questions or get them to work hard by summarizing the key points from the lesson. Target individuals or pairs, or pick pupils at random from the register. To show your picking methods are fair, write each pupil's name on a piece of card at the beginning of the year. Each time you want to choose a class member, shuffle them like a pack of cards before asking a volunteer to choose a card from the pack. Once a pupil has been chosen, leave their card out of the pack until you've been through all the cards. Keeping the pupils on their toes and telling them to expect the unexpected means they should all attempt the questions or summaries in case they're picked.

Another method is to choose one pupil to be the teacher for the last 5 minutes of the lesson, where they have to present a summary to the rest of the class. Letting them use your board and desk is often enough of an incentive to encourage them to talk to the whole class.

QUIZ VARIATIONS

WRITTEN HOMEWORK

Many of the tasks in Section 4 would make suitable homework tasks. In this case, the lesson would consist of gathering evidence and information and analysing sources that can be used in the homework task. Guide the pupils as you work through the sources, showing them how it could be useful for their homework task. This way, you're encouraging them to think independently and training them to be on the lookout for useful information and ideas.

Sometimes homework can be as simple as providing them with a series of questions to answer, all contained on one photocopied sheet. If they have time to start the questions in class, you may well need some extension work for the more able, because they will usually work quicker and end up with less homework, whereas it's exactly this group that you should be stretching with more demanding work.

Don't expect every pupil to have equal access to computers outside of school. Your school may have an ICT suite that the pupils can use for homework, but allow enough time for children to access and use it. If you expect a piece of homework to be typed up, then you must provide access to PCs for the pupils that don't have them at home.

Encourage independent learning by making the most of your school library. Setting a piece of research for homework comes with the bonus that you don't have to mark it, but the pupils should still be accountable and prove that they've completed the task. You could do this orally, asking the pupils to show and tell what they found out, or by writing a report on how they researched the topic, how successful their methods were and what they'll do next time to carry out research more efficiently. Sometimes children think that entering a word into an Internet search engine and then printing off a page of results constitutes a piece of research, but if you anticipate this problem you can avoid it. Tell them up front about the validity of information from the Internet, and the need to read and understand the research they've done. To avoid cases of plagiarism, from the Internet or from library books, ask them to present their research in a different format, such as a diagram or mind-map.

Another way to include research as homework is to give them a list of questions to which they must find out the answers. Help them out if need be by giving them the appropriate library book title or website address. If you want them to use the library, make sure you request that the book is put in the reference section so that it can't be taken out.

RESEARCH FOR HOMEWORK

The value of money throughout the ages

GENERAL TIPS ABOUT MONEY

Government documentation, such as the National Curriculum orders, suggests that financial capability can be developed through history. Very often, sources will mention an amount of money, and it can be tricky to gauge if that amount is large or small if it's not one of your areas of specialty. After all, accounts and banking have a 5,000 year history, starting in Mesopotamia, and the first known coins originate in the seventh century BC in Asia Minor. There's a lot to know about!

As historians know, it's not simply a case of translating the sum into its present day equivalent, as money had different meanings and emphases for different groups of people in the past. In addition, inflation meant prices could vary wildly even over a few decades. There are websites that claim to convert amounts from their historical worth into a present day amount, and these may suffice as an answer for curious pupils even if the formulae they use are simplistic.

It may not answer all the questions you're asked about money, but this section should give you some idea of the value of money in some of the most commonly studied past periods. Bear in mind that the figures are generalizations for the benefit of school history; those in pursuit of more accurate information could set up a research project among pupils. There are myriad websites run by universities, historical and scholarly societies and enthusiastic amateurs which will produce tables of figures concerning wages and household expenses. Use a search engine and the key words 'cost of living' along with the period you're studying. For a history of money, invest in a copy of *A History of Money: from ancient times to the present day* by Glyn Davies (Cardiff: University of Wales Press, 2002).

If you're making a newspaper front page the pupils will often want to know how much their newspaper would have cost. You can avoid this by leaving off the price altogether, or choose from some of the following advice.

THE ANCIENT GREEKS

Coins were minted in Greece in the sixth century BC. Before this, iron spits or nails were used as currency. Later there were bronze coins, some coated in silver. Alexander the Great stated that ten units of silver equalled one of gold. Six silver *obols* were worth one silver *drachma*.

THE ANCIENT EGYPTIANS

Before Greek control (end of the fourth century BC), Egypt used grain as a form of money as well as precious metals.

THE CELTS

The ancient Britons used sword blades as currency before minting gold coins. The earliest examples originate from around 125 BC. There were also silver coins and small low value coins, known as *potin*, made from copper and tin. Cattle and crops were also used in exchanges.

THE ROMANS

The Romans started off with bronze bars and began issuing silver coins in the third century BC. Values vary depending on the time and location. Augustus reformed the Roman monetary system with new gold, silver, brass and copper coins.

In Britain, Roman coins were used mainly to pay soldiers and to collect taxes. You can use this as a rough guide: one of the smallest units was an *as* (plural *asses*). Ten asses were a *denarius*. Twenty-five *denarii* made one gold *aureus*. The coins were used in Roman Britain until just after the Roman withdrawal in AD 410.

THE ANGLO-SAXONS

For a couple of hundred years, Britain reverted to the bartering system. Later Anglo-Saxon coins at first copied continental versions. In the sixth and seventh centuries, coins were minted again, being used for ornaments at first. There were no English coins found on the Sutton Hoo burial ship, although foreign coins were found.

The early silver coins are called *sceattas*. The word *sceat* originally meant 'treasure'. In the eighth century these were replaced by the silver penny.

However, not all areas of the island used coins; in Wales cattle were used as a form of money until the fourteenth century in some situations.

After preventing a total Viking invasion, in 928 Athelstan passed a law stating that there should be only one single type of money or currency in England, which exists to this day.

THE VIKINGS

Danegeld is the name for payments that English kings paid to Vikings to leave them alone; an early protection racket! The Vikings began to settle in England in 865 and established the Viking kingdom of York in 876. The coins, silver pennies, are one of the few sources of evidence which have survived about the kingdom.

THE INCAS, AZTECS AND MAYA

The Incas didn't use money although they had lots of gold and silver. Before the Spanish arrived, the Aztecs and Maya used gold dust as currency, which they kept in transparent quills. For large payments they used cocoa beans stored in sacks of 24,000.

Here is a rough guide to help you with some of the
awkward questions pupils can often ask!

THE MIDDLE AGES

A well-known coin of the Middle Ages is the *groat*. It was
introduced by Edward I in 1279 but was initially too
valuable for everyday use and so was withdrawn until the
time of Edward III, during the mid-fourteenth century.
Edward I also introduced the *halfpenny* and *farthing*, as
a penny would be a typical day's pay and smaller coins
were needed.

THE TUDORS

Henry VII introduced the English *pound* as a coin (rather
than just an accounting figure) in 1489. He introduced
the *shilling* coin in 1504.

THE STUARTS

The first British cheque that we know about was issued
in 1659. Banknotes started to be used around this time
too. *Guineas*, initially worth a pound (later 21 shillings),
were issued in 1663.

The Bank of England was founded in 1694, with the
Bank of Scotland founded the following year. After the
Act of Union with Scotland in 1707, the United
Kingdom had a single currency. The Scottish currency
abolished included the Scottish penny, the *bodle* (2
pennies), the *plack* (2 bodles), the *bawbee* (3 bodles),
the *shilling* (2 bawbees) and the *merk* (13s 4d).

INDUSTRIAL BRITAIN

At the end of the eighteenth century, a shortage of
copper and silver coins in Britain meant that many firms
had to use payments in kind, such as foreign coins and
unofficial tokens.

The gold standard was established in 1816. A new
British one pound coin made of gold was produced
called the *sovereign*. Silver pennies were no longer issued
from 1820. In 1849 the two shilling *florin* was

introduced, also known as the two bob bit. The groat was worth four pence and was last used in 1855.

TWENTIETH-CENTURY BRITAIN

In 1914 new ten shilling and pound notes were issued, and gold was withdrawn from circulation. Postal orders were made legal tender. The currency was decimalized in 1971.

Pounds, shillings and pence were the basic currency of Britain, generally expressed as '£' 's' 'd'. The pound sign stands for *librum* (plural *libra*), a pound weight in Latin, the 's' is an abbreviation for shilling (or *solidus*) and the 'd' stands for *denarius* (plural *denarii*), a Roman coin.

○ There were 12 pence to a shilling – although historically, this varied.
○ There were 240 pence to a pound.
○ There were 20 shillings to a pound.
○ A guinea was usually 21 shillings.
○ A merk was 13 shillings and 4 pence.
○ A noble was 6 shillings and 8 pence.
○ A crown was 5 shillings.
○ A half crown was 2 shillings and 6 pence.
○ A florin was 2 shillings.
○ Other coins were: sixpence, 3 pence, 2 pence, halfpence and farthings (quarter of a pence). These had various names.

On 15 February 1971, Britain decimalized its currency, meaning there were now 100 pence to the pound. Pound coins were issued in 1983 and pound notes stopped being issued in 1988, except in Scotland.

PRE AND POST DECIMALIZATION

At your fingertips

However much of a history buff you are, most people have some gaps in their knowledge. If this applies to you, then you'll find this list of monarchs and dates to be of use when researching or planning for lessons, or even when an astute pupil puts you on the spot! The list starts with Edward the Confessor's reign, as this is the point at which secondary school pupils normally start their study of history. Also included are the Scottish kings and Welsh rulers from around the same time.

HOUSE OF WESSEX, RESTORED

Edward, the Confessor	1042–66
Harold II	1066

NORMAN LINE

William I, the Conqueror	1066–87
William II, Rufus	1087–1100
Henry I	1100–35
Stephen	1135–54
Empress Matilda	1141

PLANTAGENET, ANGEVIN LINE

Henry II	1154–89
Richard I, the Lionheart	1189–99
John	1199–1216
Henry III	1216–72
Edward I, Longshanks	1272–1307
Edward II	1307–27
Edward III	1327–77
Richard II	1377–99

PLANTAGENET, LANCASTRIAN LINE

Henry IV, Bolingbroke	1399–1413
Henry V	1413–22
Henry VI	1422–61, 1470–71

PLANTAGENET, YORKIST LINE

Edward IV	1461–70, 1471–83
Edward V	1483
Richard III	1483–85

HOUSE OF TUDOR

Henry VII	1485–1509
Henry VIII	1509–47
Edward VI	1547–53
Lady Jane Grey	1553
Mary I	1553–58
Elizabeth I	1558–1603

HOUSE OF STUART

James I	1603–25
Charles I	1625–49

THE COMMONWEALTH

Oliver Cromwell	1649–58
Richard Cromwell	1658–59

HOUSE OF STUART, RESTORED

Charles II	1660–85
James II	1685–88

HOUSE OF ORANGE AND STUART

William III, Mary II	1689–1702

HOUSE OF STUART

Anne	1702–14

HOUSE OF BRUNSWICK, HANOVER LINE

George I	1714–27
George II	1727–60
George III	1760–1820
George IV	1820–30
William IV	1830–37
Victoria	1837–1901

HOUSE OF SAXE-COBURG-GOTHA

Edward VII	1901–10

HOUSE OF WINDSOR

George V	1910–36
Edward VIII	1936
George VI	1936–52
Elizabeth II	1952–present

KINGS OF THE SCOTS

Duncan I, the Gracious	1034–40
Macbeth	1040–57
Lulach, the Simple	1057–58
Malcolm III, Canmore Bighead	1058–93
Donald III	1093–94
Duncan II	1094
Donald II (jointly)	1094–97
Edmund (jointly)	1094–97
Edgar	1097–1107
Alexander I, the Fierce	1107–24
David I, the Saint	1124–53
Malcolm IV, the Maiden	1153–65
William I, the Lion	1165–1214
Alexander II	1214–49
Alexander III	1249–86
Margaret, the Maid of Norway	1286–90
Interregnum	1290–92
John Balliol	1292–96
Interregnum	1296–1306
Robert I, the Bruce	1306–29
David II	1329–32
Edward Balliol	1332–38
David II (again)	1338–71
Robert II	1371–90
Robert III	1390–1406
James I	1406–37
James II	1437–60
James III	1460–88
James IV	1488–1513
James V	1513–42
Mary Queen of Scots	1542–67
James VI (who became James I of England and Wales)	1567–1625

RULERS OF WALES

Gruffudd ap Llywelyn (of Gwynedd)	1039–63
Rhys ap Tewdwr (of Deheubarth)	1075–93
Gruffudd ap Cynan (of Gwynedd)	1081–1137
Owain Gwynedd	1137–70
Lord Rhys Overlord of Wales	1170–97
Llywelyn the Great	1196–1240
Dafydd ap Llywelyn	1240–46
Llywelyn II	1246–82

QUICK GUIDE TO NATIONAL CURRICULUM LEVELS

A copy of the National Curriculum for history will explain what a pupil needs to do to attain any of the levels, but here's a shorter way of checking their progress. It is highly recommended that you consult the official level descriptors for important assessments, as each level requires the completion of a number of skills, not just the summary mentioned here.

o Level 1: Acknowledgement of past in own and others' lives.
o Level 2: Basic knowledge with simple observations from sources.
o Level 3: Recall and describe events, people and changes.
o Level 4: Description in own structured work with correct terminology.
o Level 5: Apply knowledge and judge sources' values.
o Level 6: Critically evaluate sources and analyse own work.
o Level 7: Carry out independent research and reach own conclusions.

For those with higher level skills, some curricula allow Level 8, as well as the category of 'exceptional performance'.

At Key Stage 1, most pupils will work between Levels 1 and 3. Most should be at Level 2 when aged 7.

At Key Stage 2, most pupils will work between Levels 2 and 5. Most should be at Level 4 when aged 11.

At Key Stage 3, most pupils will work between Levels 3 and 7. Most will reach Level 5 or 6 when aged 14.

These are very rough guides of limited information: just enough to help you guesstimate the cost of a newspaper for a writing task! For more accurate information about specific years, the Internet has a vast amount of information. University and museum websites tend to be the most reliable.

ANCIENT GREECE

Day's pay of a labourer:	2 obols
Day's pay for an architect at the Acropolis:	1 drachma (6 obols)

THE ROMANS

Soldier's pay in the time of Emperor Augustus 27BC–AD14

Private:	225 denarii per year
Centurion:	3,750 denarii per year

Soldier's pay in the time of Emperor Caracalla AD211–217

Private:	750 denarii per year
Centurion:	12,500 denarii per year

FOURTH CENTURY AD

1 pair of fashionable shoes:	150 denarii
1 pair of women's boots:	60 denarii
1 pound pork:	12 denarii
1 pound beef:	8 denarii

THE MIDDLE AGES

Prices depended on availability, for example whether there had been a good harvest or not. The prices of animals depended upon their age and size. In the case of cats, their value doubled from 2d to 4d once they had killed a mouse! Many goods were not bought, but produced within households.

DURING THE REIGN OF EDWARD I

An ox:	10–12s
A lamb:	10–12d
A goose:	3d
A duck:	1d
20 eggs:	1d

FOURTEENTH CENTURY

A pound of dried fruit:	1–4d
Wine per gallon:	4–8d
A pair of shoes:	4–6d

TUDORS AND STUARTS

This is a very rough and ready guide.

- Prices were much the same from 1400 to 1500.
- By 1540 the cost of things had almost doubled.
- By 1560 it had tripled from 1500.
- By 1600 it had more than quadrupled.
- By 1620 it was five times more than 1500.
- By 1640 it was almost five and a half times that in 1500.
- Prices dropped slightly around 1680.
- By 1700 prices were almost six times the cost of things in 1500.

The average daily wage for a labourer in the 1500s was 5d and in the 1600s 1s.

ELIZABETHAN TIMES

Prices would obviously depend on the quality of the item, but you could use these as examples.

To furnish your house (from an inventory of a farm labourer):

A bowl, dishes and pair of bellows:	1s
Brass objects – basin, three kettles, a pot, two pans, two candlesticks:	16s
Pewter objects – two bowls, four plates, a saucer, a salt cellar:	5s, 4d
Plain bedstead, flocked bolster and coverlet:	12s
Old bedstead, a chest, a tub:	3s
One cow and two young bullocks:	£2, 10s
Annual income of a substantial merchant:	£100 or more
Annual wage of a maid:	£4, or less
Weekly wage of a carpenter:	5s

Sugar:	half a crown
Raisins and currants:	6d
Ginger:	1d per ounce
Loaf of bread:	3–4d
Good pair of boots:	£4–10

The average cost of running a Tudor nobleman's household for one year was about £1,000.

STUART TIMES: 1625

A pound of best cheese in the shop or market:	2½d
A quarter of best lamb:	1s, 4d
A pound of tallow candles made of wick:	4d
A vacant or empty room, either a stable or chamber by the week:	4d
One suit of cloth:	15s
One suit of canvas:	7s, 6d
Boots for men, one pair:	9s
A small kettle:	10s

1700s

Coal for a day:	one penny
Loaf of bread:	one penny
Supper of bread, cheese and beer:	3d
A pound of cheese:	4–6d
A pound of hair powder:	5d
Cost of sweeping a chimney:	6d
Turnpike toll for a carriage and four horses:	8d
A pound of butter:	8–10d
Dinner of beef, bread and beer, plus tip:	a shilling
A pound of perfumed soap:	a shilling
Tax per window of a house with 12 or more windows (1762):	1s, 6d
A stout pair of shoes:	7s
Weekly wage of an unskilled labourer:	9s
Cost of Dr Johnson's dictionary in 1756:	10s
Weekly wage of a journeyman tradesman (1777):	18–22s
A pair of velvet breeches:	£1, 10s
Annual pay of a ship's boy:	£2, 10s
Annual pay of a housemaid:	£6–8
Annual pay of a footman:	£8
Renting a house for a year:	£10
Amount needed to keep a family per year:	£40

VICTORIANS

Prices varied dramatically between the goods available for different classes of people. Most textbooks about the period discuss prices, so here are some wages of people you may study.

MID-NINETEENTH CENTURY

Annual pay of a vicar:	£40–50
Weekly wage of a London labourer:	20s
Annual pay of an engineer:	£100
Annual pay of a housemaid:	£11–14
Annual pay of a cook:	£11–50
Annual pay of a valet:	£60

LATE NINETEENTH CENTURY

Annual pay of a housemaid:	£12–22
Annual pay of a valet:	£70

BEGINNING OF THE TWENTIETH CENTURY

Figures for the twentieth century are much more readily available, so for quick reference:

Three pounds of sugar:	5d
Half pound of tea:	8d
One pint of beer:	2d
Daily wage for a labourer:	4–5s